HAZARDS OF THE DARK ARTS

MAGIC *in* HISTORY
SOURCEBOOKS SERIES

HAZARDS OF THE DARK ARTS
Johannes Hartlieb and Ulrich Molitoris

The Magic in History Sourcebooks series features compilations and translations of key primary texts that illuminate specific aspects of the history of magic and the occult from within. Each title is tightly focused, but the scope of the series is chronologically and geographically broad, ranging from ancient to modern and with a global reach. Selections are in readable and reliable English, annotated where necessary, with brief contextualizing introductions.

SERIES EDITORS
RICHARD KIECKHEFER,
Northwestern University
CLAIRE FANGER,
Rice University

HAZARDS OF THE DARK ARTS

ADVICE FOR MEDIEVAL PRINCES ON WITCHCRAFT
AND MAGIC

Johannes Hartlieb's
Book of All Forbidden Arts (1456)
and
Ulrich Molitoris's
On Witches and Pythonesses (1489)

Translated by
RICHARD KIECKHEFER

The Pennsylvania State University Press
University Park, Pennsylvania

Library of Congress
Cataloging-in-Publication Data

Names: Kieckhefer, Richard,
    translator. | Hartlieb, Johann,
    active 1450. Puoch aller verpoten
    kunst, ungelaubens und der
    zaubrey. English. | Molitor, Ulrich,
    active 1470–1501. De lamiis et
    phitonicis mulieribus. English.
Title: Hazards of the dark arts : advice
    for medieval princes on witchcraft
    and magic : Johannes Hartlieb's
    Book of all forbidden arts (1456)
    and Ulrich Molitoris's On witches
    and pythonesses (1489) / translated
    by Richard Kieckhefer.
Description: University Park,
    Pennsylvania : The Pennsylvania
    State University Press, [2017] |
    Series: The magic in history
    sourcebooks series | Includes
    bibliographical references and
    index.
Summary: "English translations of
    two important fifteenth-century
    writings on witchcraft by Johannes
    Hartlieb and Ulrich Molitoris.
    Introduction discusses the
    writings, the authors, their
    historical environments, the ways
    they used sources, and their
    influence on the development of
    ideas about witchcraft"—Provided
    by publisher.
Identifiers: LCCN 2017006833 |
    ISBN 9780271078403 (pbk. : alk.
    paper)
Subjects: LCSH: Witchcraft—Early
    works to 1800. | Magic—Early
    works to 1800.
Classification: LCC BF1569 .H3913
    2017 | DDC 133.4/3—dc23
LC record available at
    https://lccn.loc.gov/2017006833

The Pennsylvania State University
Press is a member of the Association
of American University Presses.

It is the policy of The Pennsylvania
State University Press to use
acid-free paper. Publications on
uncoated stock satisfy the minimum
requirements of American National
Standard for Information Sciences—
Permanence of Paper for Printed
Library Material, ANSI Z39.48–1992.

10 9 8 7 6 5 4 3 2

CONTENTS

ILLUSTRATIONS

All of the figures are from Ulrich Molitoris, *De laniis et phitonicis mulieribus* (Reutlingen: Johann Otmar, ca. 1489). Reproduced with permission of the Newberry Library.

ACKNOWLEDGMENTS

For help with this translation project I am indebted to Barbara Newman, to the press readers, and to the staffs of the Northwestern University Library and the Newberry Library.

ABBREVIATIONS

CIC   Emil Friedberg, ed., *Corpus iuris canonici*, 2nd ed., 2 vols. (Leipzig: Tauchnitz, 1879–81)

HDA   E. Hoffmann-Krayer and Hanns Bächthold-Stäubli, eds., *Handwörterbuch des deutschen Aberglaubens*, 10 vols. (Berlin: Walter de Gruyter, 1927–42)

HMES   Lynn Thorndike, *The History of Magic and Experimental Science*, 8 vols. (New York: Columbia University Press, 1923–58)

JH-1914   Johann Hartlieb, *Buch aller verbotenen Kunst*, ed. Dora Ulm (Halle: Niemeyer, 1914)

JH-1989   Johann Hartlieb, *Das Buch aller verbotenen Künste, des Aberglaubens und der Zauberei*, ed. and trans. Falk Eisermann und Eckhard Graf (Ahlerstedt: Param, 1989)

PL   *Patrologia Latina*, 221 vols. (Paris: Migne, 1841–55)

SH   Vincentius Bellovacensis, *Speculum quadruplex, sive Speculum maius*, vol. 4 (1624; repr., Graz: Akademische Druck- und Verlagsanstalt, 1965) (*Speculum historiale*)

SM   Vincentius Bellovacensis, *Speculum quadruplex*, vol. 3 (1624; repr., Graz: Akademische Druck- und Verlagsanstalt, 1964) (*Speculum morale*)

SN   Vincentius Bellovacensis, *Speculum quadruplex*, vol. 1 (1624; repr., Graz: Akademische Druck- und Verlagsanstalt, 1964) (*Speculum naturale*)

UM-1997   Ulrich Molitoris, *Schriften*, ed. Jörg Mauz (Constance: Verlag am Hockgraben, 1997)

Introduction

When prosecution for witchcraft first became vigorous in late medieval Europe, it was churchmen, especially inquisitors and theologians, who played the most prominent role in promoting witch trials—but laymen played an important part as well.[1] Town governments tried people as witches. Kings and princes sometimes took part in the prosecution. Even when Church courts condemned witches, the convicts were released to secular authorities for execution. But not everyone cooperated: some rulers were skeptical about the reality and danger of witchcraft, and some actually dabbled in the occult arts, or consulted astrologers and magicians whose activities seemed similar to those of witches.[2] Rather than collaborating in persecution, such rulers were (in the eyes of the zealous) negligent or even complicit. Johannes Hartlieb and Ulrich Molitoris were fifteenth-century German laymen who addressed these issues in their writings. Both of them studied in Italy, whether medicine or law, then returned to their German homelands, entered into the service of territorial princes, and endeavored to persuade these secular rulers that witchcraft and magic were serious offenses they should be vigorously uprooting. Both authors wrote as laymen, for laymen, even if their ideas were

1. Richard Kieckhefer, "The Role of Secular Authorities in the Early Witch-Trials," in *Hexenprozess und Staatsbildung / Witch-Trials and State-Building*, ed. Johannes Dillinger, Jürgen Michael Schmidt, and Dieter R. Bauer (Bielefeld: Verlag für Regionalgeschichte, 2008), 25–39.

2. The problem was of long standing; see John of Salisbury, *Frivolities of Courtiers and Footprints of Philosophers*, bk. 1, chap. 13, trans. Joseph B. Pike (Minneapolis: University of Minnesota Press, 1938), 44–54; and Edward Peters, *The Magician, the Witch, and the Law* (Philadelphia: University of Pennsylvania Press, 1978).

largely borrowed from churchmen. Their writings were grounded not only in biblical, theological, and legendary sources but also in medical and legal literature, and in the case of Molitoris they were tinged with Humanist learning. They demonstrate how late medieval witch-hunting engaged a coalition of clergy and laity, Scholastics and Humanists, molded by the cultures of northern and southern Europe, steeped in both academic and popular discourse. Lay authorities could ignore the counsel and continue to dabble and connive—as could clergy. But the task Hartlieb and Molitoris undertook was to address laymen as laymen and win them to the cause.

They had predecessors who had written for the instruction of rulers. Educated people had often cultivated favor and sought to wield influence at court. Books called "mirrors for princes" were generally meant for young and presumably malleable princes needing guidance on how to rule wisely before they had to assume the throne.[3] There were also authorities in various fields who wrote more specific advice literature on particular topics of concern to kings, including matters such as monetary policy.[4] The works of Johannes Hartlieb and Ulrich Molitoris, whole moralizing in the tradition of mirrors for princes, fall more clearly into the category of specific advice literature.

There was also, by the time Hartlieb and Molitoris wrote, a significant tradition of literature touching on the nature and perils of superstition, magic, and witchcraft. Writings describing and condemning magic can be traced back to early Christian centuries, and the work of Saint Augustine had lasting influence on such literature. Fundamental to these writings was the belief that magic was invented by demons, taught by demons, and worked with the aid of demons.

3. Georg Strack, "Piety, Wisdom, and Temperance in Fifteenth-Century Germany: A Comparison of Vernacular and Latin Mirrors for Princes," in *Princely Virtues in the Middle Ages, 1200–1500*, ed. István Bejczy and Cary J. Nederman (Turnhout: Brepols, 2007), 259–80; Cary J. Nederman and Kate Langdon Forhan, eds., *Readings in Medieval Political Theory, 1100–1400* (Indianapolis: Hackett, 2000);

Geoffrey Koziol, "Leadership: Why We Have Mirrors for Princes but None for Presidents," in *Why the Middle Ages Matter: Medieval Light on Modern Injustice*, ed. Celia Martin Chazelle (London: Routledge, 2012), 183–98.

4. The *"De Moneta" of Nicholas Oresme and English Mint Documents*, trans. Charles Johnson (London: Nelson, 1956).

When the magician wrote obscure words on a talisman, or inscribed them on the leaves of a healing plant, or wove them into a charm, they served as communication with demons—even if the magician supposed they tapped hidden powers ("occult virtues") within nature, or sought to engage the beneficent aid of unfallen angels. Superstition might be a less serious offense than magic, but it, too, came under scrutiny. The boundaries between magic and superstition were fluid, but in general the latter was a broader category. For the theologians, superstition was an offense against faith: something could be superstitious because it addressed God and the saints but in an unauthorized and inappropriate manner, or because it paid honor to creatures that should be paid only to God. From a rational skeptic's perspective, a superstition was an offense against reason: it found significance and causality where there was none, perhaps in the chattering of birds or the observance of pointless rituals.

In earlier periods magic was discussed mostly in writings that touch on it along with other issues, but in the fourteenth and especially fifteenth centuries there were numerous works devoted specifically to magic and witchcraft. Works on witchcraft began to proliferate in the 1430s, representing witches as making an explicit pact with the Devil, seeking the aid of demons, and associating with other witches in a conspiracy against Christendom. In the consolidation and spread of this concept, witchcraft trials and witchcraft literature worked hand in hand: writings about witchcraft stimulated witch trials, which led to further literature. The best known and most influential of late medieval treatises on witchcraft, the *Malleus maleficarum* ascribed to Heinrich Kramer and Jakob Sprenger, first published in 1487, was based largely on Kramer's experience as an inquisitor in southern Germany, and in response to skepticism and resistance Kramer had experienced in his prosecution of alleged witches.[5] Although Kramer was a friar and inquisitor, he shared with Hartlieb and Molitoris the project of persuading secular authorities that witchcraft was real, that magic was inherently harmful, and that lay rulers should join with inquisitors in the eradication of these threats rather than standing in the way.

5. Christopher S. Mackay, ed. and trans., *Malleus maleficarum*, 2 vols. (Cambridge, UK: Cambridge University Press, 2006), 1:103–21, has reasserted the joint authorship of the work.

JOHANNES HARTLIEB (CA. 1400–1468) AND
THE BOOK OF ALL FORBIDDEN ARTS

Hartlieb's *Book of All Forbidden Arts* is a more or less systematic treatise devoted to the dangers of superstition and magic.[6] Two circumstances are of particular importance for our understanding Hartlieb. First, he enjoyed a highly varied educational background. He obtained a bachelor's degree in 1432, a master's by 1437, and a medical doctorate at Padua in 1439. He spent time in Vienna and was steeped in the pastoral approach to theology cultivated there; he could have entered the clergy but opted not to do so. Second, he spent most of his adult life in service to princes. His father had been in service to the duke of Bavaria-Ingolstadt. He himself served the duke of Austria in his thirties, then spent much of his career at the court of Duke Albrecht III of Bavaria-Munich, and after Albrecht's death he became physician to Duke Sigmund.

Alongside his interest in medicine and theology, Hartlieb had a long-standing interest in the occult. In the 1430s and 1440s he seems to have written works on divination by various means: by phases of the moon, by consultation of names, by geomancy and palmistry.[7] The princes with whom he associated shared an interest in or apprehension for the occult arts. Duke Albrecht's mistress (and possibly his first wife), Agnes Bernauer, had been executed by drowning for sorcery in 1435, and Hartlieb's wife, Sibilla, has been identified as her daughter. One of Hartlieb's acts of service to the duke was negotiating

6. The text is edited in JH-1914 (for this and all subsequent abbreviations, please consult the list of abbreviations in the front matter); the original appears along with a modern German translation in JH-1989. For secondary literature, see especially Frank Fürbeth, *Johannes Hartlieb: Untersuchungen zu Leben und Werk* (Tübingen: Niemeyer, 1992); but also Wolfram Schmitt, *Magie und Mantik bei Hans Hartlieb* (Vienna: Notring der Wissenschaftlichen Verbände Österreichs, 1966); Christa Tuczay, "Johann Hartlieb," in *Encyclopedia of Witchcraft: The West-* *ern Tradition*, ed. Richard M. Golden, 4 vols. (Santa Barbara, CA: ABC-CLIO, 2006), 2:475; and *HDA*, vol. 3, cols. 1491–93. I follow Fürbeth in using the name Johannes, rather than Johann or Hans.

7. Frank Fürbeth, "Das Johannes Hartlieb zugeschriebene *Buch von der Hand* im Kontext der Chiromantie des Mittelalters," *Zeitschrift für deutsches Altertum und deutsche Literatur* 136 (2007): 449–79; and Johannes Hartlieb, *Kräuterbuch*, ed. Gerold Hayer and Bernhard Schnell (Wiesbaden: Reichert, 2010).

an attempted marriage alliance with the family of Margrave Johann "the Alchemist" of Brandenburg-Kulmbach. It was for that margrave that Hartlieb wrote his most famous work, *The Book of All Forbidden Arts*, in 1456, the same year in which he told Duke Albrecht in a letter about the margrave's fascination with the occult.

Apart from chapters on the Devil's powers and general warnings against the occult, *The Book of All Forbidden Arts* is organized as a survey of seven occult arts. The first of these he calls *nigramancia*, or the black art, which he clearly conflates on the one hand with classical necromancy, and on the other hand with witchcraft.[8] As he saw it, this art chiefly entails ritual magic designed for conjuring evil spirits. The second through fifth of the arts are named for the four elements—earth (geomancy), water (hydromancy), air (aeromancy), and fire (pyromancy)—following a set of categories going back ultimately to the classical writer Varro.[9] The sixth is chiromancy or palmistry, while the seventh is spatulamancy, or divination through inspection of bones. All these designations are construed broadly; aeromancy, for example, includes observation not only of birds' flight and signs in the heavens but even such things as how people sneeze, while pyromancy is defined broadly enough to include the inspection of anointed fingernails. The work is quite loose in its structure, at times almost haphazard. At one point Hartlieb seems to suggest he will go on to discuss eighty-three further occult arts, but he does not do so in the book as it comes down to us.

Hartlieb's attitude toward the occult arts is problematic. On the surface, he writes as a rationalist condemning the folly of magic and superstition, and as a moralist railing against their immorality. He tells

8. On the ambiguity of "necromancy" and "nigramancy," see Kieckhefer, *Forbidden Rites: A Necromancer's Manual of the Fifteenth Century* (Stroud, UK: Sutton, 1997; University Park: Penn State University Press, 1998), 19n14; Jean-Patrice Boudet, *Entre science et nigromance: Astrologie, divination et magie dans l'occident médiéval, XIIe–XVe siècle* (Paris: Publications de la Sorbonne, 2006), 92–94; and JH-1989, 148–49. The term "dark arts," popular-ized by the Harry Potter series, was known much earlier; it is found, for example, in David S. Schaff, *Demonology and the Dark Arts in the Middle Ages* (Lancaster, PA: s.n., 1902); and in Drahcid (a pseudonym for Bernard Wilets), *The Dark Arts: A Brief Study of Black Magic* (Long Beach, CA: n.p., 1956).

9. Friedrich Pfister, "Zur Geschichte technischer Ausdrücke in der Wahrsagekunst," *Oberdeutsche Zeitschrift für Volkskunde* 7 (1933): 44–55.

a great deal about them, but he does not write fully enough to provide actual instruction, and he repeatedly warns Margrave Johann against his temptation to dabble in such affairs. Yet historians have wondered about Hartlieb himself. He knew too much about magic to be immune from suspicion that he had tried his own experiments. As has been mentioned, writings on lunar astrology, geomancy, divination by names, and chiromancy are ascribed to him. How can he have written such things when in *The Book of All Forbidden Arts* he so vigorously condemned them? Three interpretations present themselves. First, the works of occult lore represent an earlier phase of his life and career (the 1430s and 1440s), while *The Book of All Forbidden Arts* (of 1456) comes from a time when he had been converted to a more cautious and orthodox approach. Second, it is possible that the attributions are false: that he did not write the earlier books, although he may have copied some such works in full or in part simply to inform himself more fully of their contents. This argument is more plausible for some of the writings in question (e.g., the work on geomancy) than for others (e.g., the treatise on chiromancy). Third, he may just have been ambivalent. For all his condemnatory bluster, he clearly was fascinated by the occult, immersed himself in it, wanted to know how it worked, and he may have dabbled in its use more than he was willing to admit. Frank Fürbeth, who has written most extensively on the matter, sees Hartlieb as drawing on a tradition of moral and catechetical literature—indeed, as contributing significantly to a thriving tradition of moral instruction—that does not show he had been an offender, and yet suspicions will linger.[10]

The idea that there are seven occult arts is modeled on the notion of seven liberal and seven mechanical arts. There had been various categorizations of magic in medieval sources. Isidore of Seville in the seventh century gave an untidy list of the forms of magic, devoted mainly to means of divination or fortune-telling. He had shared and popularized Varro's idea of geomancy, hydromancy, aeromancy, and

---

10. Fürbeth, *Johannes Hartlieb*, esp. 109–27; but see also Bernhard Schnell, "Neues zur Biographie Johannes Hartliebs," *Zeitschrift für deutsches Altertum und deutsche Liter-* *atur* 136 (2007): 444–48. And in the treatise itself see chapters 2 (ambiguous reference toward the end), 33–34, 37b (especially important, but again ambiguous), 56, 107–8.

pyromancy as among the branches of magic, corresponding to the four elements earth, water, air, and fire, and many writers adopted this fourfold schema, but what else counted as magic varied a great deal.[11] Isidore included necromancy, which he still took in its classical sense, meaning telling the future by conjuring the spirits of the dead. By the later medieval period "necromancy" or "nigramancy" (no clear distinction was made) was understood as conjuring demons, whether to tell the future or for other purposes, and this was the first of Hartlieb's seven occult arts, in some ways the most important. Some classifiers had mentioned chiromancy, but Hartlieb was unusual in highlighting this as one of the seven major arts. Even more unexpected was his granting this status also to spatulamancy. In any case, Hartlieb did not observe his categories rigorously; they provided a framework to which anything he wished to discuss might be attached.

His explicit sources are of three basic sorts. First, he was clearly familiar with the writings of the magicians, although he cites these mainly in his account of necromancy or "nigramancy" (chaps. 23, 26, 27, 28, 30, 35, 36), and he does not have a great deal to say about the actual content of these writings. Second, he draws widely on ecclesiastical and medical sources—theologians such as Thomas Aquinas, medical writers such as Galen—and here he does give actual content. Yet he can be frustratingly vague at times, as when he cites "the doctors of holy Scripture" (chap. 11). Third, he refers to his own personal experience: to a trial in Rome involving people who changed into cats and went about killing children (chap. 33); to a case in Heidelberg in which he interrogated an accused witch (chap. 34); to an incident in which he interviewed a woman who practiced palmistry (chaps. 106–8). He tends to describe these personal testimonies at some length, and with an attention to detail he clearly relished. Apart from these three types of explicit source, Hartlieb makes considerable use of lore for which he does not cite a source, and which he could have learned either from

11. Lynn Thorndike, "Some Medieval Conceptions of Magic," *The Monist* 25 (1915): 107–39; William Klingshirn, "Isidore of Seville's Taxonomy of Magicians and Diviners," *Traditio* 58 (2003): 59–90; *The "Etymologies" of Isidore of Seville*, bk. 8, chap. 9, trans. Stephen A. Barney, W. J. Lewis, J. A. Beach, Oliver Berghof, and Muriel Hall (Cambridge, UK: Cambridge University Press, 2006), 181–83.

reading or from oral accounts: he speaks of an unguent made with seven plants plucked on particular days (chap. 32), of bread and cheese used for fortune-telling (chaps. 50–51), of different ways to obtain water for hydromancy (chap. 58).

Hartlieb has much to say about the practitioners of magic and superstition, who came from all ranks of society (chap. 2). To be sure, some forms are more common among the lower classes: it is "old women" who engage in certain forms of hydromancy (chaps. 60–61), belief in changelings is found more among women than men (chap. 129), and Hartlieb knows the reputation of Gypsies for palmistry (chaps. 103–4). Still, he knew princes and lords who made use of superstition in hunting (chap. 69), courtiers who wore superstitious feathers without realizing the practice is superstitious (chap. 70), even a great prince who used an executioner's sword for divination (chap. 88). The general movement was from lower to higher classes. Thus the custom of fortune-telling by means of the breastbone from a goose eaten on Saint Martin's Day was once practiced by old peasants on remote farms, but then it spread among royalty and nobility, even high clergy. Even when the princes were not themselves practitioners, they bore responsibility for what was done in their lands, and Hartlieb scolds them for their negligence in suppressing infidelity: practitioners of magic and superstition proliferated in German lands because the princes tolerated and protected them, although a truly faithful prince should help root them out (chap. 79a).

Hartlieb's book is full of moral exhortation (throughout, but especially chaps. 17, 119, 123, 126). He speaks often of the Devil, the "founder and inciter" of the arts of fortune-telling (chap. 68), who involves himself in forms of divination that one might think innocuous (chap. 117). The Devil's powers are limited, but he is clever about getting around the barriers he confronts: he cannot coerce people's minds or senses, but he beguiles them successfully (chap. 118). Hartlieb was fond of the thirteenth-century Cisterian monk Caesarius of Heisterbach, whose *Dialogue of Miracles* was an important source of anecdotes about the supernatural events that happened not long ago and not far away. He even wrote a German translation of portions from Caesarius's compilation.[12] When he cites Caesarius in his *Book of All Forbidden Arts*, it is always in the context of human dealings with the Devil: he tells stories from Caesarius illustrating the danger of taking counsel from the Devil (chaps. 12–16), or the risk of being damned for association with the Devil (chap. 29a), and in one case the story he borrows is about a monk who in death escaped from the clutches of the Devil (chap. 95). He is aware that certain magicians thought they were invoking not the Devil but holy angels for their magic; like other critics, he held this to be an illusion, because the "angel" these masters invoke "is really a devil" (chap. 92).

The "forbidden arts" described in this book are, from Hartlieb's perspective, offenses against the faith. The term he usually uses for them is *unglouben*, not simply superstition in a modern rationalist sense but unbelief. At one point he refers to a form of fortune-telling that leads people to suppose their children or their horses have been cursed, and he speaks of that practice as a heresy (chap. 127), and he refers to the goose bone used in fortune-telling as a "heretical superstition" (chap. 130). He tells of superstitions linked with popular observance in Christmastime, traceable to archaic pagan practice (chap. 64). He speaks of superstitions involving the perversion of the Church's sacramentals: water blessed for the feast of Saint Blaise (chap. 65). Elsewhere he speaks of sorcerers who sprinkle the blood of birds as sacrifice to spirits of the air (chap. 78), or who use wax images for sorcery (chap. 78), and in his account of pyromancy he refers several times to the use of an innocent child as a divinatory medium (chaps. 83, 84, 88, 89, 90).

The text as we have it breaks off abruptly and is clearly incomplete, either because Hartlieb did not finish it or because of problems in transmission. The former explanation is more plausible, because

12. His German translation of Dist. 7–12 is in *Johannes Hartliebs Übersetzung des "Dialogus miraculorum" von Caesarius von Heisterbach, aus der einzigen Londoner Handschrift*, ed. Karl Drescher (Berlin: Weidmann, 1929). There is a modern English translation, Caesarius of Heisterbach, *The Dialogue on Miracles*, trans. H. von E. Scott and C. C. Swinton Bland, 2 vols. (London: Routledge, 1929). *HDA*, vol. 2, cols. 10–16, calls attention to aspects of the work that are relevant to Hartlieb.

the work seems in general rather hurriedly put together, and there is no reason to think the author ever devoted time to its careful revision. The work did not enjoy any particular success; Hartlieb asked the margrave to share it with his friends, but we have no concrete evidence that this happened, and there are only three manuscripts in existence. Still, it gives a fascinating picture of the practices Hartlieb found rife in the society of his time—and of his vigorous if somewhat ambivalent efforts at reform.

ULRICH MOLITORIS (CA. 1442–1507) AND
THE DIALOGUE *ON WITCHES AND PYTHONESSES*

Ulrich Molitoris's *On Witches and Pythonesses* (1489) is a dialogue on the powers and culpability of witches.[13] Molitoris is also known, if rarely, by the vernacular version of his name, Müller, but the Humanist preference for the invariant Latin genitive "Molitoris" (referring in principle to his father's trade as miller) shows even in the German version of his dialogue published not long after the Latin original, where he is called Ulrich Molitoris. He was a much younger contemporary of Hartlieb, and the difference in their age correlates with differences in cultural context. Molitoris had Humanist leanings, studied at the Humanistically inclined University of Pavia, and wrote among other things a comedy in Latin. Back in German territory, he entered into service to Archduke Sigismund of Austria in 1488 and later became chancellor of the duchy of Tyrol. His dialogue is dedicated to that prince, and he wrote it as part of the process of being

---

13. The Latin text of this and other works by the author is in UM-1997. There is a French translation, Ulric Molitor, *Des sorcières et des devineresses, par Ulrich Molitor, reproduit en fac-similé d'après l'édition latine de Cologne 1489*, presumably translated by Émile Nourry (1926; repr., Paris: Tiquetonne, 1990); and a modern German translation, Ulrich Molitor, *Von Unholden und Hexen*, trans. Nicolaus Equiamicus (Diedorf: Ubooks, 2008). For secondary literature see Jörg Mauz, "Ulrich Molitoris aus Konstanz (1442–1507): Leben und Schriften" (PhD diss., University of Constance, 1983); Jörg Mauz, *Ulrich Molitoris: Ein süddeutscher Humanist und Rechtsgelehrter* (Vienna: Schendl, 1992); and Edward Bever, "Ulrich Molitor," in *Encyclopedia of Witchcraft*, ed. Golden, 3:776–78.

considered for ducal service. It takes the form of a dialogue involving three speakers. In his own person he quotes from a relatively wide range of sources, and he is almost the only one to refer to canon law. The magistrate Conrad Schatz, a municipal judge at Constance, had experience in trials for sorcery, and in the course of the dialogue he draws on his judicial experience, giving an account that is partly corroborated by surviving archival evidence (chap. 5). When he draws on tradition, he cites the Bible and legends of the saints more often than he does more erudite sources. Archduke Sigismund plays the skeptic and mostly urges the other speakers along with brief interventions and queries, to which sometimes Ulrich and sometimes Conrad responds. In the later portions of the dialogue, which I am labeling Part II, issues that have been freely discussed are meant to be resolved; Conrad drops out of the exchange, and Molitoris himself is the main speaker, taking clear charge of responding to the archduke's questions.

Archduke Sigismund, whom Molitoris served, and to whom he dedicated his dialogue, was a figure of some importance in the history of witchcraft and witch-hunting. He ruled over Tyrol (including Innsbruck) and "Further Austria," a cluster of territories around southwestern Germany. In 1485, the inquisitor Heinrich Kramer (or Institoris) conducted extensive prosecution for witchcraft in Innsbruck, and some of the accused had links to the archduke's court.[14] Sigismund at first lent Kramer the support he owed to a papal inquisitor, and may actually have been convinced that witch-hunting was necessary. The trial eventually foundered on procedural and other grounds, and the archduke drew back from his initial support. Kramer went on to write the *Malleus maleficarum*, the best-known treatise

14. Heide Dienst, "Lebensbewältigung durch Magie: Alltägliche Zauberei in Innsbruck gegen Ende des 15. Jahrhunderts," in *Alltag im 16. Jahrhundert: Studien zu Lebensformen in mitteleuropäischen Städten*, ed. Alfred Kohler and Heinrich Lutz (Vienna: Verlag für Geschichte und Politik, 1987), 80–116; Richard Kieckhefer, "Magic at Innsbruck: The Case of 1485 Reexamined," in *Religion und Magie in Ostmit-* *teleuropa: Spielräume theologischer Normierungsprozesse in Spätmittelalter und Früher Neuzeit*, ed. Thomas Wünsch (Münster: Lit Verlag, 2007), 11–29; Manfred Tschaikner, "Hexen in Innsbruck? Erzherzog Sigmund, Bischof Georg Golser und der Inquisitor Heinrich Kramer (1484–1486)," *Der Schlern* 88 (2014): 84–102. Christopher Mackay is currently working on the documents related to this trial.

on witchcraft from the fifteenth century, and in that work he urged
that secular authorities should join in the prosecution of witches.
Sigismund remained cautious and wanted further counsel on the
matter, which Molitoris was pleased to provide for him in the form of
his dialogue.

Coming out only two years after the *Malleus maleficarum*, Molitoris's work takes a more nuanced approach to the topic than does the
Malleus. He recognized the witches' allegiance to the Devil as a reality, and also sex with the Devil in the form of an incubus. He viewed
the Sabbath, the witches' flight to the Sabbath, and metamorphosis
into animal form as ultimately dreams or illusions. The error in such
matters is one about fact: what the witches think happens does not in
fact happen. With the Devil's help, witches can practice weather
magic, love magic, sorcery to cause bodily harm, and divination. Here,
on Molitoris's reckoning, the error is one not of fact but of cause: the
bewitchments do in fact occur, but the witches are wrong in believing
they cause them; at most it is the Devil who brings them about, with
God's permission. Implicitly disagreeing with the *Malleus*, Molitoris
does not accept the notion that witchcraft represents a new sect, a
conspiracy against Christendom involving nocturnal assemblies of
witches and demons, but he does believe that as individuals witches
turn against God, ally themselves with the Devil, bring harm to others,
and are thus deserving of execution. While he does not deny the
competence of ecclesiastical tribunals to prosecute witches, he speaks
only about the role of secular courts—those for which the archduke
had responsibility, and in which Molitoris himself had witnessed how
witches are tried.

The chapters of the dialogue deal with weather magic, sorcery to
cause bodily harm, magically induced impotence, transformation of
humans into other the forms of animals, magical transport to the
witches' assembly (he calls their *convivium*, their assembly or entertainment, what other writings call the Sabbath), whether witches can
have sex with the Devil in the form of an incubus, whether children
can be born of such copulation, whether fortune-telling women can
know future and secret things with the aid of demons, and how
witches should be punished. Under some but not all these headings
Molitoris speaks of evidence taken from trials: from the confessions

of witches, and from the accusations made against them, or rumors of the sort that became matter for accusation. That witches can influence the weather and cause bodily harm is a common report, corroborated by confessions of accused witches. That witches have had sex with the Devil is also affirmed by confessions.

In each section of the dialogue Sigismund typically raises objections: surely confessions under torture are worthless; rumors can be woefully misleading; only God controls the weather and knows the future; the famous canon *Episcopi*, which had been issued by an early medieval synod and incorporated in canon law, denied the possibility of transformation into animal form and of flight in the company of malign spirits. Molitoris does not give extended theological response to such objections, as the *Malleus maleficarum* had done. Some of the objections are glossed over without serious consideration, such as the challenge to testimony given under torture. In other cases Molitoris makes or implies distinctions: transformation of substance from a human into an animal is impossible (as the canon *Episcopi* rightly says), but changes in sense impressions can be worked in various ways, most of which involve illusions caused by the Devil. By far most often, Molitoris draws on scriptural, historical, literary, and legendary sources to show that what witches are alleged to do is indeed possible, with demonic aid: demons can afflict people, they can make plausible conjecture about the future, they can make humans seem to become animals, and so forth, all of which is amply shown by sources in which Molitoris placed great trust. For example, the story of the Swan Knight, which became the basis for Wagner's *Lohengrin*, serves as an authority for the notion that intercourse with demons can produce offspring. At one point the skeptical voice in the dialogue protests, "You are telling a fable! The poets invented things that are not to be believed." The response comes from Lactantius: that the poets were writing histories veiled beneath hidden figures (*sub occulto figmento*), which is to say there was a core of truth beneath the cloak of fiction.

The title of Molitoris's dialogue requires comment. It refers to witches as *laniae*, and fortune-tellers as *phytonicae mulieres*, pythonic women or pythonesses. Both terms are feminine. As Molitoris surely knew, *lamia* was a term used in classical Latin for a witch, sometimes a blood-sucking witch, and its confusion with *laniare* or "tear apart" led to the form *lania*, which Molitoris himself preferred.[15] He would also have known that a pythoness was a fortune-teller such as the oracle of Delphi, where Apollo had slain Python the serpent. Molitoris was not the first to borrow such classical vocabulary: *phitonissen* for "witches" had occurred earlier in German-language trial records.[16] Still, these were not common terms, and it is a bit odd that in the title itself he equated them with the more familiar German words *unholden* and *hexen*, even though these beings were not traditionally known either for blood-sucking or for oracular prophecy. He actually uses *laniae* only in the opening sections of his work, and *phitonicae mulieres* only twice. Elsewhere his vocabulary is kaleidoscopic: he uses interchangeably *strigae* (from an Italian term for witches), *maleficae* (a generic word for malefactors or witches), *incantatrices* (enchantresses), and *maleficae mulieres* (bewitching women or sorceresses). He tends to assume that witches are mostly women, yet he does refer also to *malefici* (sorcerers), *magi* (magicians), *arioli* (male fortune-tellers), *ioculatores* (illusionists), and *mathematici* (here meaning astrologers), all in the masculine.

The linkage of classical with later Latin and vernacular terms was symptomatic for Molitoris's project, which at many points cites classical literature for the light he thinks it sheds on the witches brought to trial in late fifteenth-century Germany. He could cite the authority of Virgil's *Eclogues* and the histories of Rome. He could allude to the rhetoric of Terence. He quotes at length from Boethius on the story of Ulysses and Circe.[17] Molitoris was writing as both a lawyer and a Humanist, and while his primary audience was a prince from whom

15. UM-1997, 113n1. See also, e.g., Petrus Mamoris, *Flagellum maleficorum*, chap. 11, in *Dæmonstrix, seu adversus dæmones et maleficos, universum opus ad usum præsertim Exorcistarum concinnatum*, vol. 3 (Lyon: Bourgeat, 1669), 154: *lamia est animal furibundum, et de lamia, quasi lania, a laniando pueros* ("lamia, as if lania, from tearing children apart").

16. For *ars phythonica* and *phitonissen* in Biel (1466–67) and in

Cologne (1488–89), see Peter Joseph Kämpfen, *Hexen und Hexenprozesse im Wallis* (Stans: C. v. Matt, 1867), 15–16, 25, 49–50; and Joseph Hansen, ed., *Quellen und Untersuchungen zur Geschichte des Hexenwahns und der Hexenverfolgung im Mittelalter* (1901; repr., Hildesheim: Olms, 1963), 502–6.

17. Boethius, *The Consolation of Philosophy*, bk. 4, poem 3, trans. Richard Green (New York: Macmillan, 1962), 83–84.

he sought and obtained patronage, his broader audience was a reading public that might not be able to quote Boethius and Virgil but respected the authority of those who could. The main purpose of his classicism was to persuade these readers that belief in witchcraft could be grounded in the full range of sources a Humanist was expected to have mastered.

While Molitoris was eager to display his classical learning, the great majority of his sources are traditional Christian ones such as the Bible, legends of the saints, and Saint Augustine. His reliance on Augustine is not surprising. Augustine's defense of Christianity against pagan attacks in *The City of God* led him to vigorous assault on the magic that he saw as integral to traditional Roman paganism, and his treatise *On the Divination of Demons* is the classic medieval reference for the notion that fortune-telling can be accurate only because it relies on information obtained from cunning demons.[18] When Molitoris cites incidents from the lives of the saints, taking them as fact, he seems to rely heavily on a German translation of James of Voragine's *Golden Legend*, a thirteenth-century compilation of saints' legends and other material that had wide currency in the later medieval West.[19] He leans even more on the work of Vincent of Beauvais, a Dominican friar of the thirteenth century.[20] Vincent compiled what amounted to the greatest encyclopedia of medieval Europe, in the form of a series of *Mirrors*. His *Mirror of Nature* dealt with the entire spiritual and material world, more or less following the order

18. Augustine, *The City of God Against the Pagans*, trans. R. W. Dyson (Cambridge, UK: Cambridge University Press, 1998); *The Divination of Demons*, trans. Ruth Wentworth Brown, in Saint Augustine, *Treatises on Marriage and Other Subjects*, ed. Roy J. Deferrari (New York: Fathers of the Church, 1955), 415–40.

19. Jacobus de Voragine, *The Golden Legend: Readings on the Saints*, trans. William Granger Ryan (Princeton, NJ: Princeton University Press, 1993).

20. Cited here from *SH*. See especially Mary Franklin-Brown, *Reading the World: Encyclopedic Writing in the Scholastic Age* (Chicago: University of Chicago Press, 2012); and *HMES*, vol. 2, chap. 96, pp. 457–76; also Astrik L. Gabriel, *The Educational Ideas of Vincent of Beauvais* (Notre Dame, IN: University of Notre Dame Press, 1962); Joseph M. McCarthy, *Humanistic Emphases in the Educational Thought of Vincent of Beauvais* (Leiden: Brill, 1976); and W. J. Aerts, Edmé Renno Smits, and J. B. Voorbij, eds., *Vincent of Beauvais and Alexander the Great: Studies on the "Speculum maius" and Its Translations into Medieval Vernaculars* (Groningen: Forsten, 1986).

given in the creation narrative of Genesis 1, turning then to a quick survey of geography and history. The *Mirror of Teaching* deals largely with practical matters such as the duties of a prince and the art of warfare, the mechanical arts, medicine and law, and agriculture, the virtues, physics, and mathematics. The *Mirror of History* traced the course of history up to the year 1250. A fourth compilation, the *Mirror of Morals*, was actually not by Vincent but put together in the following century. Relying on compilations such as those by James of Voragine and Vincent of Beauvais allowed Molitoris to convey a sense of deep and broad learning, even when much of his material was taken at second hand from these compilations.

Because Molitoris had been trained in ecclesiastical or canon law, we would expect him to draw on it in his dialogue, and he does, but he shows less depth of legal learning than one might anticipate. The foundation for canon law was the *Decretum*, a massive twelfth-century compilation associated with the renowned jurist Gratian; later enactments were added, with the authority of thirteenth- and early fourteenth-century popes, but the most important canons dealing with magic and witchcraft were in the *Decretum*, particularly Part 2, Case 26, Questions 3 to 5, under which seventeen canons (drawn from various sources, especially regional Church councils and the writings of Augustine) are quoted and discussed.[21] One of these texts is the canon *Episcopi* (Question 4, Canon 12), which had been included in earlier compilations of canon law but now had the authority of Gratian behind it. This canon, named *Episcopi* because its first word is the Latin term for "bishops," begins by urging bishops and their officials to banish from their midst those guilty of fortune-telling and harmful magic. It then turns to what it claims is a widespread belief in sinful women who ride about at night on animals in the company of the goddesses Diana and Herodias. This belief is a pestiferous error, inspired by the Devil, who presents illusions of this sort to foolish women while they sleep. These are illusions of fact, not of causality. Those holding to them—not just the women who believe they do such things, but others in the general public—are not simply misled but culpable. When fifteenth-century writers developed the mythology

---

21. *CIC*, vol. 1, cols. 1024–36.

of the witches' Sabbath, and judicial authorities prosecuted people for attending the Sabbath, flying to it, forming a pact there with the Devil, and having sex with the Devil in the form of an incubus or succubus, this complex of beliefs seemed to revive precisely the error condemned by the canon *Episcopi*. Some writers argued that the Sabbath was indeed an illusion but that assent to the Devil's allurements was still culpable. Others argued that the Sabbath and associated activities were not in fact the same as what the canon took to be illusion, but something new and different. One way or another, the canon *Episcopi* was a roadblock that writers had to surmount, including Molitoris.

Molitoris's work is also important in the early artistic depiction of witchcraft. The early editions typically included a series of woodcuts. The first, not given in all printings, shows Sigismund receiving the book from Ulrich and Conrad Schatz, the participants in the dialogue. The next woodcut has a witch shooting an arrow at a man's feet to make him lame. The third in the series depicts three witches, in animal form but wearing long robes, flying on a forked stick. In the fourth, a male witch rides a wolf to the witches' assembly, although the wolf is walking on the ground and appears to be moving rather sluggishly. The fifth has a thinly disguised demon embracing a witch. The sixth and most famous shows two witches casting a cock and a snake into a seething cauldron, while a storm breaks out from a dark cloud above the cauldron. The last depicts three women seated at an outdoor meal, which can be identified only by implication as the witches' banquet; the food appears quite ordinary. Three of the images (the third, fourth, and seventh) relate to the witches' assembly, which Molitoris viewed as illusory, and thus what they depict is the witches' illusion. The fifth shows the erotic relationship between a witch and a demon, which Molitoris thought of as real, but which is here rendered in rather tame form, with both figures fully clothed and standing. The second and sixth depict bewitchments, which the text represents as reality but does not describe in detail.[22] These woodcuts

22. Natalie Kwan, "Woodcuts and Witches: Ulrich Molitor's *De lamiis et phythonicis mulieribus*, 1489–1669," *German History* 30 (2012): 493–527; Charles Zika, *The Appearance of Witchcraft: Print and Visual Culture in Sixteenth-Century Europe* (London: Routledge, 2007), 18–27.

are reproduced here from a printing done around 1489 in Reutlingen by Johann Otmar, held by the Newberry Library.

While Hartlieb's book had no broad circulation, Molitoris's dialogue did reach a considerable audience. First published in 1489, it was reprinted in 1494, 1495, and several times in the sixteenth century. By 1669 it had been printed thirty-nine times, more often than the *Malleus maleficarum*. A German translation, often taken to be by Molitoris himself, came out soon after the Latin original. Beginning in the later sixteenth century, the work was disseminated as an appendix to the *Malleus maleficarum*. The princes of late medieval and early modern Europe may have shown little interest in Hartlieb's project of reforming their own morals, but Molitoris's dialogue helped spur them to a cause in which many did become zealous: the burning of witches and ridding society of this most fatefully imagined threat.

COMPARISON OF THE TWO WORKS

The most obvious differences between Hartlieb's work and Molitoris's are in form and focus: Hartlieb wrote a vernacular survey of the forbidden arts that is on a superficial level tightly organized, while Molitoris penned a Latin dialogue on witchcraft with the more overtly rambling quality of a dialogue. Certain shared circumstances are also clear: both writers were laymen, educated partly in Italy, who served territorial princes back in Germany and wrote their works for the instruction of those princes. The two pieces are of interest as specifically lay writings, and as appeals to secular authority.

Other shared features are worth noting. First, both Hartlieb and Molitoris emphasized strongly the cunning, deceptive nature of demons: they trick people into believing they have and can impart more power than they actually have at their disposal. Hartlieb is most insistent on the seductive element in this trickery, the demons' success at winning followers by alluring them with attractive promises that lead ultimately to their perdition. The issue for him is mainly *errors of moral judgment*: demons lead people to suppose they can use magic and superstition without incurring serious harm. Molitoris has somewhat different concerns. He is more focused on the theological issue of what the witches and the demons can and cannot do, and how effects are worked. For him, what the demons induce are mainly *errors of fact* and *errors about causality*. They lead witches to believe falsely that they go, for example, to their assemblies; in fact the assemblies are pure delusion, but witches who assent to this delusion are still culpable and subject to execution. The demons also want the witches to suppose it is their rituals that cause such things as destructive storms; the storms and other bewitchments do actually occur, and the witches are rightly punished for them, but it is actually the demons themselves and not the witches' rituals that cause bewitchment to work. The difference here is one more of emphasis than of principle. Other early writings on magic and witchcraft, indeed even patristic works, also talk about the illusory dimensions of these arts, but the clear stress on the theme of delusion in the works of Hartlieb and Molitoris stems perhaps from a sense that laymen are particularly susceptible to the demons' wiles.

A second feature that these two share is a fear that the secular rulers may be lenient in their treatment of magic and witchcraft. They both wish to impress on the princes, and indirectly on a much wider audience of lay readers, that the issues must be taken seriously, that the offenses are by no means trivial. Even when witches were deluded, their delusion was culpable. No doubt there were ecclesiastical authorities who also winked at transgressions, but the danger of laxity was here ascribed mainly to lay rulers.

Third, both our authors show an eagerness to draw on the works of clerical culture—Augustine, Caesarius of Heisterbach, Vincent of Beauvais, and others—and a willingness to appropriate that work uncritically, making little distinction between legend and history, fiction and fact, folklore and literal truth. If such distinctions arise, they are quickly set aside. Lay Christians in the fifteenth century were increasingly asserting their own authority in religious matters, all the way from the parish level to that of high ecclesiastical politics. But they did not always base their claim to authority on distinctly lay viewpoints or traditions. Rather they could claim—as Hartlieb and Molitoris in effect did—that they had equal access to and mastery of the same sources that churchmen commanded.

In the end, Hartlieb and Molitoris demonstrate that the distinction between clergy and laity, which from a sacramental perspective had the clarity bestowed by holy orders, was not absolute from a social or cultural viewpoint. Hartlieb had an education that a priest might also have had, and at one point he came close to being ordained and accepting a position as parish priest at Ingolstadt, but instead he remained lay and married. Molitoris studied canon law and might easily have moved into a position in ecclesiastical administration but instead remained a layman in service to laymen. The works given here in translation, then, do not represent distinctly lay approaches to witchcraft and magic, but the appropriation of clerical approaches by writers who occupied lay roles, mingling and serving with the lay rulers for whom they articulated the views they shared with many clergy. They served as channels through which these views were taken over from a clerical into a lay sphere, and they show laymen asserting a kind of moral authority that might earlier have seemed more specifically clerical. It is for that reason that they are particularly interesting and important.

NOTE ON THE TEXT

In the translation of Hartlieb, the section letters A through M are the translator's insertions, as are the section headings for B through M. Chapter designations for that work are insertions by the editors or the translator in the cases of chapters 1, 29a, 37a–c, 39a, 79a, and 124–132. In the translation of Molitoris, the designation of parts I and II is an insertion by the translator, as is the use of numerals for the individual questions, and in the case of question 3 also the question heading.

The Book of All Forbidden Arts

JOHANNES HARTLIEB

A. THE PROLOGUE TO *THE BOOK OF ALL FORBIDDEN ARTS, SUPERSTITION, AND SORCERY*

Chapter 1

O eternal wisdom of the divine majesty, source of all created things, shining light and right compass of the true way to everlasting blessedness, from which spring and flow grace, salvation, fortune, reason, and mastery of all arts, grant me, Doctor Hartlieb, a sharing in your wisdom and counsel, help and teaching, so that I may write down and assemble the countless superstitions which with clever tricks of deception are carried out with pretense of goodness, bringing frequent dishonor and despite to your Holy Trinity. For you, the divine and everlasting being, are the true creator and cause of all things, and without your grace nothing can exist or be fulfilled, and so many a person errs and goes astray who honors and prays to your creation and handiwork rather than to you. Satan, the archenemy of the whole human race, who devises and discovers thousands of means for guile, incites and aids and misleads people in this direction. He does so to deceive, delude, defraud, and debauch the children of man, who have been formed and fashioned in your image, and have been saved and redeemed by God's bitter passion and by the shedding of his holy blood.

Chapter 2

Such sorcery, superstition, and devilish phantoms have unfortunately become rooted and implanted in the hearts of many people of high and low status. I am thus willing to write at the request, urging, and

commission of the illustrious, highly praised prince, Margrave Johann
of Brandenburg, a veritable lover of true and proper arts, and a man
filled with pity for those who have gone astray.[1] And [I do this] so that
all Christian people may be on guard against these things, and may
pursue only those forms of art and mastery which lie hidden within
nature and are allowed by the Christian Church. So much art and
beauty are veiled therein, for the delight of bodies, souls, and minds,
that there is no need to pursue or to uphold the forbidden arts and
superstitions, with which beyond all doubt we grievously enrage the
divine majesty. Noble, highborn prince and brother-in-law, son of the
most Christian prince Margrave Friedrich,[2] a true lover of all clergy
and worthy priesthood, since your high understanding so eagerly
craves, seeks, and investigates all arts and occult lore, and nothing is
lacking to your utter perfection but knowledge of the Latin language,
it would be utterly lamentable if your profound wisdom were ensnared,
entrapped, or enmeshed in the cunning of sorcery and superstition.
For that reason I, Doctor Hartlieb, am gathering material and writing
for my all-gracious lord and brother-in-law, dealing in the first place
with the seven forbidden arts, namely, nigramancy, geomancy, hydromancy, aeromancy, pyromancy, chiromancy, and spatulamancy. After
that I will deal with all other such superstitions and phantoms of the
Devil, which through all my days I have heard read out, told, and
practiced. And I ask Your Grace to share the book with all your good
friends, because it will surely cause many evil customs and superstitions to be despised and renounced.

Chapter 3

Genuine Christian faith is a true light to the soul and leads to our final
desire, eternal life. When we have attained it, we experience peace and

1. This is, however, Johann "the
Alchemist" to whom Hartlieb is
referring.
2. Friedrich I, margrave and elector
of Brandenburg (reigned 1417–25),
father of Johann. The latter was not lit-
erally Hartlieb's brother-in-law; JH-1989,
145; Wolfram Schmitt, *Hans Hartliebs
mantische Schriften und seine Beein-
flussung durch Nikolaus von Kues* (Stuttgart: Paul JLLG, 1962), 70, 212–13.

rest—but otherwise never, for we stand always amid cares. The person with true faith should avoid all superstition, sorcery, and specters of the Devil, and should flee and avoid all forbidden arts. For the thousandfold cunning artist has innumerable tricks and arts with which he deceives, deludes, and defrauds people, in particular those who are frivolous, simple, and weak in mind and have love only for earthly and transient things, lightly despising what is eternal and perduring. Shedding light on such matters is a great concern among doctors of divine Scripture, who bring enlightenment to holy Christendom. They discuss whether the Devil with his phantoms and illusions can incite and lead people to evil or good; whether the Devil can give good counsel, encouragement, and aid; and whether one should follow him and whether humans should undertake his service.

B. POWERS OF THE DEVIL

Chapter 4: What right faith is, and what benefit comes from it

Since the setting forth of argument and counterargument reveals and makes clear the underlying truth of any matter, it is appropriate to set forth both sides on this matter and then to uphold the truth. First of all, the Devil cannot introduce or force anything into the mind, soul, or understanding of any person, for God has made human beings noble and exalted, according to his image and likeness, so that no phantoms of the Devil can force their way in unless a person lends his will to this. Or, from another perspective: if the Devil could force or compel a person's mind, then the person could do nothing other than what the Devil wills.

Chapter 5: That the Devil cannot compel a person either to good or to evil

Since the Devil always and in every case works only evil and no good, a person would then be unable to do any good; but that is not the case, because a person has his free will, to do evil and good. Thus it is not

right for a person to act according to the counsel or instigation of the
Devil. The other side of the matter is this: if the Devil were to give
good counsel or do some good service, why should a person not follow
him? As the highly learned Seneca says, "Do not heed who speaks,
heed only what is spoken."[3] If then the Devil counsels something that
is good, why should one not follow him? Or, from another perspective:
A person may take aid and counsel from evil, wicked humans, so why
should he not accept a good service from a devil?

Chapter 6: That no one can request counsel of the Devil without great mortal sin

The final answer of holy Scripture to this argument and counterargument is, in short, that no one should seek or accept counsel, help or
guidance, service or support from the Devil. For although a person
may have good in mind, the Devil is so rich in cunning that he does
nothing but set traps and snares for humans, in which he can ensnare
and bind them. One must therefore be on guard against the evil spirits, for in truth the Devil is a father of all lies and evil [John 8:44]. And
anyone who is so gullible as to believe in his aid and counsel can
through his great shrewdness and cunning become unable to flee and
escape from ever more disgrace, derision, and damage. No one can
accept service and counsel of the Devil without great sin. It is written
in [II] Kings [1:2–17] that the king of Israel was much punished and
tormented for seeking counsel of the idol [at] Ekron.[4] Thus anyone

---

3. Perhaps Seneca, *On Tranquil-
lity of Mind*, chap. 11 ("I shall never be
ashamed to quote a bad author if what
he says is good"), in Seneca, *Moral
Essays*, trans. John W. Basore, vol. 2
(London: Heinemann; New York: Putnam, 1932), 258–59, or his twelfth letter to Lucilus ("so that all persons who
swear by the words of another, and put
a value upon the speaker and not upon
the thing spoken, may understand that
the best ideas are common property"),

or the sixteenth ("Whatever is well
said by anyone is mine"), in Seneca,
Ad Lucilium epistulae morales, trans.
Richard M. Gummere, vol. 3 (London:
Heinemann; New York: Putnam, 1917),
72–73, 106–7.

4. The reference is to King Ahaziah
(or Ochozias), king of Israel ca. 870–ca.
850 BCE, accused of venerating Baal-
Zebub (Beelzebub), the god of Accaron
(Ekron).

who takes or receives service or counsel from the Devil creates for himself great trouble and in any case commits a mortal sin. Therefore, esteemed prince, take pains to avoid all this.

Chapter 7: How certain things are allowed to the Devil, and why God so allows

There are many further questions: how the Devil deceives frivolous people, how he possesses them, how the Devil allures and deceives people. Your Grace will find all that below in what is written about superstitions. But in the end you should know that the Devil cannot beguile, deceive, or tempt anyone unless that person yields his will thereto, or unless it comes of God's dispensation, which is hidden to all persons. Yet Bonaventure and Saint Thomas [Aquinas] say in the eighth distinction and in the first question that God grants the Devil power over no one unless to reveal his glory or to punish sins and the sinner, or to make manifest the deeds of divine honor.[5] The reasons for what happens are hidden from the children of men, because the judgments of God are concealed, yet they are not unjust. One must understand that the Devil cannot beguile, deceive, or lead anyone astray by his own power, against that person's will. Thus, O highborn prince, give your will to none but God, and so all devils must flee from you.

Chapter 8: Whether the Devil knows the thoughts of the heart

Again, there is a question whether the Devil knows and understands the thoughts of people's hearts. The holy doctors answer that the Devil cannot know the thoughts of any person. This matter involves a great deal of argument and counterargument that I will forego, because it is of no particular use to laymen.

5. JH-1989, 140, 153–54; JH-1914, lxi–lxii, points out that the reference is actually to Thomas Aquinas, *Summa theologiae*, pt. 1, qu. 114, art 1.

Chapter 9: A lesson in how one can resist the Devil

Sometimes frivolous people will say, "I am so much and so often beset by the evil devils that I am afraid I cannot resist them." But as Saint Jerome says, this only shows a frivolous spirit and a dull disposition. There is also a question, whether the devils know future things. Holy Scripture answers that the essential nature of the devils has not been taken from them, rather divine grace is removed from them.[6]

Chapter 10: How some things are natural, and some are from the Devil

One must know that certain things are future and must happen because they have their own causes and cannot happen otherwise, such as an eclipse, or the rising of the sun each morning. The devils can know about these things, as do people such as stargazers. Then there are things that are future such as the growth of fruits and grain, that are variable, so no one can know them fully, neither the Devil nor a human, but only God. There are also things that are matters of "no" and "yes," such as everything within the scope of human free will. These no one can know but God alone. You should also note, my most gracious lord and brother-in-law, that many stargazers presume to answer all questions; their folly and ineptitude in this regard is worthy of harsh punishment, as Your Grace will hear and note further on when I write about the mantic art.[7]

Chapter 11: Whether the Devil should be followed if he gives good counsel

Another question to decide is this: whether one should follow the Devil and accept his service if he counsels, guides, or gives aid to

6. The references both to Jerome and to Scripture are too vague to allow precise identification of the source.

7. JH-1914 notes that the passage at the end of the chapter is unclear in all three manuscripts.

someone in good, honorable activities. The opinion of the doctors of holy Scripture is that no one should receive or accept counsel or guidance, aid or instruction from the evil spirits, because the Devil is so hateful and inimical to all the children of man that he is bent at all times on setting pitfalls and traps for humans, misleading and misguiding them. He may do a few things that prove good and useful to those who believe in his specters, but he does that only to induce trust in him and his cunning, to mislead and misguide people in the end.

C. AN EXAMPLE FROM CAESARIUS OF HEISTERBACH

Chapter 12: A good example about the Devil and about correct faith

We read in Caesarius [of Heisterbach]'s *Book of Dialogues of Miracles* how a knight fought with two counts, carrying on a deadly war.[8] The force of the counts overwhelmed the knight, so that he suffered much loss to his retinue and his goods. The knight was thus without a squire.[9] A comely young man came and said to the knight, "Lord, if you wish to have my service, I will serve you gladly and truly." The knight took him into his service. The young man was so eager to serve that the knight never mounted or dismounted without the squire holding his stirrup. There were countless other services that he more than other people performed for his lord. The knight developed great trust in this squire, for in all the time he served him, the knight prospered in all things.

---

8. Free adaptation of book 5, chap. 36, in Caesarius of Heisterbach, *Dialogue on Miracles*, trans. Scott and Bland, 1:366–68.

9. The text has *knecht*, "servant," following Caesarius's Latin original, which uses *servus* (three times), but the context justifies Eisermann and Graf's translation *Knappe*, referring more specifically to a squire.

Chapter 13: How the Devil and the knight went riding by themselves

Once the knight took the young man alone by himself to find out the position and makeup of his enemies. The enemies came against him. They chased the knight and his squire, closing in on them so tight that he was forced up against a great river. The knight said to the young man, "Now we will soon be dead, since we have no more aid or comfort." The squire said, "Lord, be of good cheer—I know a good crossing through the water, on which I have often ridden." The knight said, "My dear squire, there has never been a crossing through the river." The squire said, "My lord, I will ride on ahead." Mortal peril compelled him; the knight followed the squire. Soon they made their way across the river with no trouble at all. The enemies soon arrived on the scene and marveled at his squire, yet he kept silent about the situation.

Chapter 14: How the knight's wife became ill

Soon afterward the knight's wife became deadly ill. Wise physicians were called in, but with their arts all they could determine was that the woman would die the next morning. They told that to the knight. The woman was given all the Christian rites. The knight paced grief-stricken about the chamber. That struck pity in the squire, who went to his lord and said, "My dear lord, what is troubling you that you are so anxious and forlorn?" The knight said, "O dear, faithful squire, you cannot console me, for my wife, in whom all my comfort lies, is going to die in the morning, as the wise doctors say." The squire said, "My dear lord, let me too visit my lady and see if I can provide her with any counsel or aid." The lord led the squire to his consort.

Chapter 15: How the Devil gave counsel about the woman's illness

The squire felt her pulse, then called the knight to the doorway, and said, "O lord, my lady has a burning fever. If she could take lion's milk, she would at once recover." The knight exclaimed, "O dear squire, now you have brought me even deeper distress! Where could we obtain lion's milk, since there is no lion living for miles around?" The squire said, "If you wish, I can bring lion's milk quickly." The lord spoke like a person caught in grief, and said, "Yes!" The squire took a vessel and came back in three hours, bringing lion's milk. He slathered it on his lady, and at that very hour the woman recovered. She went to her lord and comforted him. The knight was joyful and sent for the young man, saying, "My dear squire, tell me now, where did you obtain lion's milk so quickly?" The young man said, "Lord, I knew a lioness in Arabia who is giving suck to twelve cubs, and I milked her and brought the milk." The lord said, "My dear squire, how do you travel so fast, when Arabia is many hundred miles from here?" The squire said, "Lord, why do you ask? My lady is well!"

Chapter 16: How the knight asked the Devil who he was and what his nature was

The lord said, "Dear squire, I must ask you on your oath who you are." The young man said, "I am your faithful squire." The lord said, "I adjure you by God and his holy passion to tell me who you are!" The young man said, "My lord, I am a devil." The lord said, "Now tell me what your reward is to be. I may not and will not retain you, since my faith forbids association with devils." The young man said, "Dear lord, retain me and I will serve you faithfully, and as long as I remain with you your affairs will prosper." The lord said, "No, by no means! Tell me, what is your reward? You kept me alive at the river, and you cured my mortally ill wife. If you ask for half of what I own, I will gladly give it to you." The squire said, "My lord, retain me; I will make you abundantly rich in goods, honors, and pleasures, and will make all your enemies subject to you." The lord said, "No, by no means!" The young man said, "Lord, since you will not retain me, I ask nothing more than five shillings for all my service. Purchase a little bell with it, and when the precious elements are transubstantiated at mass, have this little bell rung, so that those passing by hear it and give praise." The lord said, "Gladly—consider it done!" At once the young man vanished.

D. MORAL EXHORTATION

Chapter 17: Good counsel on imitating this knight's honorable conduct

O noble, highborn prince and brother-in-law, take note how this Christian knight would not for any sake receive the help of the Devil, and turn yourself from all sorcery and from devilish and all forbidden arts, which are all phantoms of the Devil. Pay no attention to them, for they are nothing but trumpery. Make use of the reasoning power that God has given you, following the will of God and the natural gifts that God has given to you more than to many others. Flee from all scent of sorcery and superstition, and you will find your fortune, well-being, and happiness increased. You have faithful and pious knights and servants who protect you and your land. You have faithful subjects on the land who provide for your nourishment. You have understanding of high natural arts, more than other people, scholars and laymen. So cast away the evil specter of the Devil, and flee from the deceptions that are without number. Still, I will go on to describe for you the seven forbidden arts, which are called the necromantic, and eighty-three [further arts], which are all contrary to God and the true Christian faith.[10]

Chapter 18: How each Christian soul is wedded to God

You should know, most esteemed prince, that, as Saint William writes, the Lord God has wedded to himself each Christian soul as his true spouse, just as a man marries his wife.[11] Even if a man has no cause of

10. This sentence raises two problems: Hartlieb refers to all the seven arts (presumably including nigramancy or necromancy) as *Nigramanticas*, and he says he will describe eighty-three further arts (which he does not in fact do). The second problem could suggest an ambitious plan that was not realized, but that would not solve the first difficulty. It is only remotely possible that he thinks of the treatment of necromancy as having seven subdivisions, and that of the remaining six arts as having a total of eighty-three subdivisions.

11. Either William of Auvergne or William of Saint-Thierry; see JH-1989, 154–55.

suspicion pointing to adultery, still he is solicitous about his wife, as is right. For it is not enough that a wife preserves her marital fidelity; she should also be on guard against anything that might give evil suspicion or evil semblance of adultery or infidelity. So it is, too, with God, the true knower of all hearts: he will not allow any unbelief or evil thought to come between him and his spouses and consorts.

Chapter 19: How the Devil enters into people and possesses them

Finally, let us take up briefly the question how the Devil possesses people and misleads their minds and senses. Your highly cultivated reason should take note that the Devil cannot and may not constrain any person's mind, but he entices a person with evil appearances and images. As soon as a person yields his will to these, the Devil presents the illusion of all those things in which a person takes delight, and he guides and teaches and gives aid in their pursuit. Then the person's will becomes so attached that he can never get loose. You can see how this works in proud persons, whose pride increases because the devil of pride has possessed them. So, too, with the avaricious—their avarice does not abate, because the Devil of avarice has possessed them.

Chapter 20: Another example showing how to avoid sin

Your Grace may take a lesson from all unchaste women and men. Alas, how often one finds men and women who break their marital fidelity with people who are much less attractive in body and in appearance than their proper spouses. No matter how great the disgrace and disrepute they incur, they cannot desist. The cause is that their minds and senses are afflicted and possessed by the evil devils of unchastity. The Devil thus possesses all who are held and hardened in such sin and disgrace. How wonderful it would be if all nobles were free and innocent of such misdeeds, for then the common people would desist from these and other sins.

Chapter 21: An example and teaching about fleeing and avoiding evil customs

Believe me, esteemed prince, many common people are misled and misguided by the evil example of nobles, and the nobility must and will atone for this. Guard yourself against this, esteemed prince, and lead your life in such a way that all your subjects will improve themselves following your example. That will be the greatest treasure you can leave behind yourself.

E. NIGRAMANCY (NECROMANCY)

Chapter 22: The first art, nigramancy, which is called the Black Art

Nigramancy is the first forbidden art, and it is called the Black Art.[12] This art is the worst of all, because it involves sacrifice and service that one must do to the devils. One who wishes to work with this art must give various types of sacrifice to the devils, and must make vows and compact with the devils. For the devils are thus obedient to him and fulfill the will of the master [i.e., the magician], as far as God allows. Take note of two great evils in this art. The first is that the master must give his sacrifice and tribute to the devils, with which he denies God and renders to the devils divine honor. For we should offer sacrifice only to God, who created us and redeemed us with his passion. The second is that he binds himself with the Devil, who is the greatest enemy of all humankind.

---

12. *HDA*, vol. 6, cols. 997–1002.

13. On these sources see JH-1914, xliii–xlvii; JH-1989, 141, 144, 151, 152; *HMES*, vol. 2, chap. 49, pp. 279–85. Ulm emphasizes the difficulty of estab-

lishing exactly to what texts Hartlieb is referring (e.g., she suggests that his *Jerarchia* could refer to a writer named Hierax or Hieracas).

Chapter 23: The various things one uses in the art of nigramancy

The masters of this art need for such things various books, figures, and characters. One book they call *The Seal of Solomon*, another *The Key of Solomon*, a third *Hierarchy*, a fourth *Shemhamphoras*, and further they make use of various characters.[13] With the characters and unknown words the human binds himself with the Devil and the Devil with the human. The same literature of the evil art teaches how one can and should conjure the Devil with the characters and secret words. But all that is mere trumpery, since there is nothing in nature that can coerce or compel spirits, as holy Scripture says.

Chapter 24: How one sets out learning the art of nigramancy

One who wishes to set out in the teaching and school of the Black Art finds in the same book many secret and unknown words that are not taught in any [other?] writing;[14] and he knows how one is to say these words devoutly, while using suffumigations and burning various aromas and sacrificing various animals. With these words the human gives himself body and soul to the evil Devil. With the incense and sacrifice he scorns God and gives divine honor to the Devil, his great enemy. On account of such great sin God then grants to the Devil that sometimes the master's will comes about, [thus ensnaring the magician].

Chapter 25: How the Devil deceives and deludes his master in the Black Art

The Devil acts toward his master as though coming to him brings him great suffering, and he cries out loudly, "Oh, you cause me such great

---

14. Eisermann and Graf reverse the order of chapters 23 and 24, on the not implausible ground that this reference to the "same book" makes better sense that way. Their suggestion is followed here.

and grievous pain!" O poor master, how pitiably you let yourself be duped and led astray by the Devil with his thousand deceits! He acts as though he felt suffering and pain from your conjuring and exorcising—but far from it, he takes great joy and pleasure in this: he rejoices that he has taken and withdrawn your soul from God almighty. In this way you are misled and brought to eternal torment.

Chapter 26: Certain books about the Black Art

There are several books about the art that teach how one is supposed to conjure and exorcise the devils with plants, stones, and roots, such as the book *Kiranides*, which teaches how to put plants, stones, fish, and birds together in a metal container suited for that purpose.[15] With that one is supposed to obtain great things from the Devil. All that is superstition, and the Devil involves himself in it and leads astray all those who believe in it. For you can be sure of this, that all the power of nature is small in comparison with the power of the devils, let alone that of the good angels, as Job [41:25] says: "There is no power on earth that can compare with the devils." You might say, "But in [the book of] Tobias [6:1–9, 7:11, 8:1–3] one reads that the liver of a fish, placed on a glowing coal, drives away all devils." Consult on this the appropriate gloss of Nicholas of Lyra, and also Saint Thomas; it says there that it is not the smoke of the liver but the devout prayer of the youth Tobias that drove the devils from Raguel.[16]

Chapter 27: More books of the Black Art

There are still more books on this art, such as Thabit [ibn Qurra], Ptolemy, Leopold of Austria, Arnold, and all the books that have been

15. *HMES*, vol. 2, chap. 46, pp. 229–35; Maryse Waegeman, *Amulet and Alphabet: Magical Amulets in the First Book of "Cyranides"* (Amsterdam: Gieben, 1987).

16. Nicholas of Lyra, *Postilla super totam Bibliam*, vol. 3 (1492; repr., Frankfurt am Main: Minerva, 1971), sig. Dv^r, col. a.

written about images,[17] which are many, telling how one at any particular time should fashion an image of the planets and stars, which have great power for love and harm, victory and fortune.[18] All that is trumpery, for it involves a great deal of secret words, and characters and suffumigation and sacrifice, which is all unchristian. But there is a book called *De annullis inpensis* that is ascribed to Arnold of Villanova, which teaches great things, but they are all mingled with superstition.[19] Albert and Thomas also wrote about images and heavenly influences, it is claimed; all that is forbidden, and in any event I do not believe that such learned doctors actually wrote about such foolishness and superstition. I firmly maintain that it is [falsely] ascribed to them, since Albert the Great wrote a book against all such forbidden books and teachings. His book begins, "On account of certain books"; one finds listed in it many of the forbidden arts and books.[20]

Chapter 28: The *Consecrated Book* in the Black Art

There is another book in this forbidden art that is called the *Consecrated Book*, and they consecrate it on the high, wild mountains.[21] All who have dealings with this book are led astray and seduced, because

17. Reading *bilden* (as further on in the chapter) for *wilden*, although the manuscripts do not show this as a variant. Eisermann and Graf translate as *Talismane*.

18. On these sources see JH-1941, xlviii–lii; JH-1989, 139, 147, 150; Francis J. Carmody, *The Astronomical Works of Thabit b. Qurra* (Berkeley: University of California Press, 1960).

19. On Arnold see *HMES*, 2:841–61; and Arnaldus de Villanova, *Epistola de reprobacione nigromantice ficcionis (De improbatione maleficiorum)*, ed. Sebastià Giralt (Barcelona: Seminarium Historiae Scientiae Barcinonense, 2005).

20. *HMES*, vol. 2, chaps. 59 and 62–63, pp. 517–92 and 692–750; Paola Zambelli, *The "Speculum astronomiae" and Its Enigma: Astrology, Theology and Science in Albertus Magnus and His Contemporaries* (Boston: Kluwer, 1992); David J. Collins, "Albertus, *Magnus* or *Magus*? Magic, Natural Philosophy, and Religious Reform in the Late Middle Ages," *Renaissance Quarterly* 63 (2010): 1–44.

21. *Liber iuratus Honorii: A Critical Edition of the Latin Version of the Sworn Book of Honorius*, ed. Gösta Hedegård (Stockholm: Almqvist & Wiksell, 2002); Claire Fanger, ed., *Conjuring Spirits: Texts and Traditions of Medieval Ritual Magic* (Stroud, UK: Sutton, 1998), 143–65.

they must give themselves to the Devil, and each one must dedicate himself to the Devil with his own blood, becoming subject to tribute. The offices of the devils are forty-six. And the master must render special sacrifice to each office. This is the most despicable book of all there is in this art. Oh, how often and how much God and his holy name are dishonored and despised therein! The same *Consecrated Book* contains all the trickery and deception found in nigramancy. The masters of the book can accomplish whatever they desire, but they do so only when God allows it. They thus squander a portion of their life,[22] and afterward they willingly go forever and eternally astray. Their sin and their despair are so great that one seldom hears of one returning to grace, so thoroughly do they despair of God. That is altogether the most evil aspect of nigramancy. If one is to interpret the word, as Isidore says, nigramancy is an art that awakens the dead, who can then tell future and past things, but he uses the word nigramancy in a general sense, touching with it many aspects of superstition and sorcery.

Chapter 29: The notary art

In this category there is also the *ars notoria*, which enables a person to learn all the arts by means of certain words, figures, and characters.[23] This art is only carried out by means of a bond with the evil devils, for the secret words bring about association and bond between the Devil and the human. Although this art entails fasting, prayer, and pure, chaste living, still it is forbidden and a sin, because beneath this show of goodness the evil devils conceal their seduction and misleading of poor humankind. Therefore, noble prince, flee from this art, for it is condemned by Holy Church.

---

22. *Sy geben ir lebtag ain zeitt,* which Eisermann and Graf construe as making implicit reference to a fixed-term pact with the Devil—a possible reading.

23. *HMES*, vol. 2, pp. 285–89; *HDA*, vol. 1, cols. 602–6; Julien Véronèse, *"L' Ars notoria" au Moyen Age: Introduction et édition critique* (Florence: Sismel, 2007).

Chapter 29a: An example

Holy Church condemns [these things].[24] In the book of miracles by
Caesarius [of Heisterbach] one reads how a black monk lay in mortal
illness.[25] He was dense and ignorant but he wanted to become learned.
The Devil came to him in his illness and said, "If you dedicate yourself
to me, I will give you this stone. If you have it with you, you will know
all arts." The monk said, "I will dedicate myself only to God." The devil
went away, but left the stone lying there. The monk picked up the
stone; he knew all arts, more than any master in Paris did. Many were
amazed at this. Soon the monk died, and he was damned. Notice here,
noble and esteemed prince, how harmful it is to have association and
dealings with the Devil.

Chapter 30: The book of Raziel

There is another book called *Liber Razielis*, which teaches many wondrous things about these arts, and makes pretense that it all involves
holy angels, for in it one has to fast, pray, and burn offerings.[26] The
pretense misleads many good Christians. O prince, I tell Your Grace
that many people place great faith in this evil superstition.[27] Your
Grace should shun the *Liber Razielis* and all the practices drawn from
it, such as the *Opus Urionis*. It is truly a mortal poison for a poor soul.

Chapter 31: Flight through the air

In this evil, wretched art of nigramancy there is a form of foolishness
that people carry out with their tricks of sorcery. Horses come into

24. This fragment is given in JH-1914, not in JH-1989.

25. Caesarius of Heisterbach, *Dialogue on Miracles*, trans. Scott and Bland, Book 1, chap. 32, 1:39–41.

26. Bill Rebiger, Peter Schäfer, Evelyn Burkhardt, Gottfried Reeg, Henrik Wels, and Dorothea M. Salzer, eds., *Sefer ha-Razim I und II: Das Buch der Geheimnisse I und II* (Tübingen: Mohr Siebeck, 2009), gives the Hebrew text with the Latin (*Liber Razielis*); see JH-1914, lii–liv; JH-1989, 151.

27. A play on *gelauben . . . ungelauben*.

an old house, and if one wishes he can mount them and ride many miles in a short time. When he wants to dismount, he holds onto the bridle, and to mount again he shakes the bridle, and the horse returns.[28] The horse is in fact really a devil. For such sorcery one needs the blood of a bat; using it, a person must devote himself to the Devil with secret words such as "debra ebra." This practice is widely known among princes. Your princely grace should shun it, for it would truly be a pity if your elevated mind should be caught up in and led astray by any such operations.

Chapter 32: How the flight through the air takes place

For such flight men and women—that is to say, the witches [*unhulden*][29]—make use of an unguent that is called *unguentum pharelis*. They make it out of seven plants, and they pluck each plant on a day that is proper to that plant. Thus, on Sunday they pluck or dig for *solsequium*, on Monday *lunaria*, on Tuesday *verbena*, on Wednesday *mercurialis*, on Thursday *barba Jovis*, on Friday *capillus Veneris*. With these they make an unguent, mixing some blood of a bird and the fat of animals;[30] but I will not write it out, lest it bring someone into trouble. When they wish, they smear this unguent on benches or chairs, rakes, or oven-forks, and they fly away. That is all true nigramancy, and it is strictly forbidden.

Chapter 33: A noteworthy case of sorcery

Honorable prince, let me tell you about a case that I saw and heard in Rome along with many other people. In the sixth year of the pontifi-

28. Kieckhefer, *Forbidden Rites*, 42–43, 54–57. Links between Hartlieb and the manuscript edited in *Forbidden Rites* would be all the more interesting if it could be established that Hartlieb actually held or consulted that manu-script, but that connection remains tantalizingly speculative (see ibid., 33–34, 37).

29. Note the explicit suggestion that witches can be of either gender.

30. *HDA*, vol. 2, cols. 1373–85.

cate of Pope Martin [V] [reigned 1417–31], there arose in Rome a superstition that certain women and men changed themselves into cats and killed many Roman children. Once a cat came into a burgher's house and bit his child in the cradle. The child cried, the father quickly got up and took a knife and stabbed the cat through the head as it tried to get out a window. Early the next morning a woman [of the vicinity] had the holy sacrament brought to her. The neighbors lamented her illness, as is the custom, and the father joined in the lamenting. She reproached him, "If you were really sorry about my sickness, you would not have done it to me." On the third day it came out that the woman had a wound in her head. The neighbor thought about the cat, and about what she had said. He brought the matter to the Senate. The woman was taken and confessed. She said out loud before the Capitol that if she had her unguent she would flee away. Oh, how I and many members of the court would have loved to see it happen, if only someone had given her the unguent! But a doctor stood up and said the unguent should not be given to her, because the Devil could bring about great disarray, with God's permission. The woman was burned, as I myself saw. And it was said at Rome that there were many such people. It was also said that some old women could have a man ride about on calves and goats. And if that is indeed so, then without doubt it is the Devil who does it, for nothing else than to seduce people and lead them astray. Your Grace may ask, "Why do old women do that more than men?" The learned masters answer that women are generally more unstable in their minds and in their faith; for that reason the Devil involves himself with them more than with men.[31]

Chapter 34: Making hail and storms

Making hail and storms is another of these arts, for someone who wishes to be involved in it must not only devote himself to the Devil

31. Cf. *Malleus maleficarum*, pt. 1, qu. 6, trans. Mackay, vol. 2, pp. 111–25.

but also deny God, holy baptism, and all Christian grace.[32] This art is done and perpetrated by no one but old women who have forsworn God. Listen and take note, O highly esteemed prince, of a significant case that I myself encountered and experienced. In the year of the Lord 1446, certain women were burned at Heidelberg for sorcery. The mistress who taught them came from there. In the following year I came on an embassy from Munich to the illustrious, highborn Duke Palatine Ludwig.[33] May God be gracious to him, for if a prince is upheld in faithfulness then he is ever with God.[34] During these same days came a rumor about how the mistress was captured. I asked his grace to let me go to her. The prince was willing. He had the woman and also the inquisitor[35] brought to me in a little town called Götsheim, where the master of his household lived, a man named Peter von Talheim.[36] I obtained from the prince the favor, that if the woman taught me how to make storms and hail he would let her live, but she would be banished from his land. When I went to the woman and the inquisitor alone in a chamber, and asked for her teaching, the woman said she could not teach me unless I did everything she taught me to do. I asked what that was, and said that so long as I did not anger God or act against Christian faith, I would do it. She lay there with one foot in an iron fetter, and she said to me, "Dear son, you must first of all deny God and pray for no more comfort or help from him. Then you must deny baptism and all the sacraments with which you have been anointed and marked. Then you must deny all God's saints, and especially his mother, Mary. Then you must devote yourself with body and soul to three devils, whom I will name for you, and they will give you a time [remaining] to live and will promise to carry out your will until

32. Note that here the masculine pronoun is used—the magician devotes *himself* to the Devil; although the German can be seen as having the equivalent of common gender, one might have expected an alternative and more specifically feminine formulation, particularly given that the rest of the chapter suggests that the practitioners are likely to be women.

33. Ludwig IV (1424–1449).

34. *wann sol ain fürst durch sein triü behalten werden, so ist er ye bey got*: Eisermann and Graf expand the text and suggest that the prince's reward is to be with God in Heaven.

35. *ketzermaister.*

36. Peter von Talheim was counselor of Friedrich I, Pfalzgraf bei Rhein (1449–1476); in 1445 he was in the retinue of Ludwig IV; see JH-1989, 153.

that time ends." I said to the woman, "What else must I do?" The woman said, "Nothing more. Whenever you want to carry out this matter, go to a secret place, call on the spirits, and sacrifice to them the N.,[37] and they will come and within an hour they will make hail wherever you want." I told the woman I would do none of this. For I had said before, if she could teach me such arts without my angering God or acting against the Christian faith I would set her free. She said she knew of no other way to do these things. The woman was again turned over the Hans von Talheim, who had her burned in the place where he had captured her. O prince, rich in virtue and honor, listen and take note what a great and serious sin this is, and wherever you come into contact with it, do not tolerate any such women. There are some people who immerse the crucifix[38] of Jesus Christ in deep water to carry out their sorcery, which is a great heresy and superstition. The Devil inspires and aids in this, in order to seduce people and lead them into eternal torment.

Chapter 35: The book *Picatrix*

There is another noteworthy book on the art of nigramancy that begins, "To the praise of God and the most glorious Virgin Mary," called *Picatrix*.[39] It is the most complete book about the art that I have ever seen. This book is was put together for a king of Spain, no doubt by an exalted doctor, for he has embellished the art with natural properties and with quotations from holy Scripture, so that many quite learned men fully believe it is no sin. The book seduces many people to eternal damnation. Your princely grace should be particularly on guard against this book, for bitter poison is mixed in among its sweet words. The book *Picatrix* is larger than three psalters. O what deceit and cunning Satan had to deploy in inspiring this book!

---

37. Presumably meaning that different terms can be inserted, depending on the desired outcome; see JH-1989, 148.

38. *marter pildt.*

39. *Picatrix: The Latin Version of the "Ghāyat Al-akīm,"* ed. David Pingree (London: Warburg Institute, 1986); *HMES*, vol. 2, chap. 66, pp. 813–24; an English translation of *Picatrix* by David Porreca is in progress. *Picatrix* in fact begins with praise of God but not of the Virgin Mary.

Chapter 36: The *Book of the Holy Three Kings*

There is another book, ascribed to the Holy Three Kings, and it begins, "There were three magi in Egypt."[40] This book also has true sorcery and superstition mixed in with clever stratagems and sayings, and throughout it all runs the art of the stars. And one who does not fully understand these things will suppose it is without any sin, so masterfully is it put together. I have seen much in this book that causes even me to wonder how it might be so true and proper. It is the Devil with his thousand deceits who does all that, to urge people on to their seduction. Your princely grace should take guard against this book, for its beginning is sweet, but its ending is a bitter eternal damnation for the soul, forever and without end.

Chapter 37: The dead head that speaks and gives answers

There is yet another evil, reprehensible deception in the art of nigramancy that involves a dead head that one conjures, with fine aromatic suffumigation and candles, and then the head gives answers to questions. O poor master of your reason and sense! You think the head answers, but it is the evil Devil within it who answers you. He often tells you what is true, to seduce and mislead you. Most gracious prince and brother-in-law, guard yourself against this evil sorcery, for I know in fact of a prince in your family who was quite seriously led astray by this practice. O prince rich in knowledge and understanding, Your Grace should know that no one can write down all the elements of the Black Art, taking into account all the many deceptions the evil devils have invented and concocted for humans.

---

40. See JH-1914, lvi–lviii; also the edition of the German translation in Bodo Weidemann, *"Kunst der Gedächtnis" und "De mansionibus": Zwei frühe Traktate des Johannes Hartlieb* (Berlin: Ernst-Reuter-Gesellschaft, 1964), 180– 93 (*De mansionibus*, or "buch der heiligen drey konig"). Note that Fürbeth, *Johannes Hartlieb*, 152, calls into question Hartlieb's authorship of the divinatory writings.

Chapter 37a: Another chapter on the punishment for the evil art

O most virtuous prince and lover of all learning! There is still another great and serious practice in the art of nigramancy, and it is like this: When a simple man is at death's door and is ready to die, someone conjures his spirit, that he will come back and serve him and remain with him for a specified number of years; and the master takes an oath and pledge of loyalty from the dying man, and conjures him with great conjurations that form part of this procedure. This practice is truly a deeply disquieting one, for who knows if it is the spirit of this same man who comes back or a devil. Myself, I believe it is a devil, who without doubt misleads the man. Even if it were the spirit, which the masters of the art call a "serving spirit," still it is a sin and forbidden. Guard yourself against this, as against a mortal poison, my brother-in-law, for you and I wish to be God's servants and not those of the Devil. Amen.

Chapter 37b: Another chapter on the punishment for the evil art

Further there is a weighty question, whether a person may call on a dying man to come within thirty days and tell him what condition he is in.[41] Your princely grace should consider well and guard yourself against that, for it is very harmful, for the Devil often involves himself in it, and as I know well. Yet certain masters say that this practice may be well, when one is seeking thereby nothing but the soul's salvation. I dare not say what I myself have researched and seen and heard, since I am still

41. Jean-Claude Schmitt, *Ghosts in the Middle Ages: The Living and the Dead in Medieval Society*, trans. Teresa Lavender Fagan (Chicago: University of Chicago Press, 1998), 137; Catherine Rider, "Agreements to Return from Afterlife in Late Medieval Exempla," in *The Church, the Afterlife and the Fate of the Soul*, ed. Peter Clarke and Tony Claydon (Woodbridge, UK: Boydell, 2009), 174–83. Hartlieb speaks of an arrangement with a dying person, not (as in Eisermann and Graf) one already dead.

in doubt.[42] But if I may give voice to safer judgment, I think the matter is entirely deceitful and is not without the involvement of evil devils.

Chapter 37c: What nigramancy and other evil superstitions are

I wish to write down for your princely grace the fundamentals, that your high understanding may well grasp what nigramancy involves. You should know, my most gracious lord and God-fearing prince, what sacrificial practices are involved: rendering living or dead offerings at crossroads, burning candles at the threshold, making suffumigations, forming characters or figures with one's own blood. All those are practices and elements of the true black art. Not only should your princely grace guard against all that as against evil venomous serpents, but you should not allow that such things be carried out and practiced in your princedom. Dear brother-in-law, guard yourself against the evil devils, and leave them to experience all misfortune, for they are God's capital enemies and ours. I hope to God that I may take vengeance on them. Give up your crystals, too, I give you my true counsel, for when I write of the fourth art of pyromancy I will explain these to you and condemn them as is necessary. Let this suffice regarding nigramancy. Now I will write about the second art, which is called geomancy in Latin and is close kin to astronomy.

F. GEOMANCY

Chapter 38: Of the second art, called geomancy, which is forbidden by Holy Church

Geomancy is a forbidden art in which the masters think they can inquire and learn about all future and past affairs.[43] This art involves

---

42. The verb *versucht*, translated here with deliberate ambiguity as "researched," does not in late medieval German *necessarily* imply that Hartlieb personally attempted magical experiments. Matthias Lexer's *Mittelhoch-*

deutsches Handwörterbuch (Leipzig: Hirzel, 1872–78) under *versuochen* gives *zu erfahren, kennen zu lernen suchen, forschen nach, prüfen, auf die probe stellen; zu erlangen od. zu tun suchen.*

43. *HDA*, vol. 3, cols. 635–47

use of earth or sand or chalk on a board, or with ink on paper, or the discernment of even or odd [numbers of] points. According to strict interpretation of the word, geomancy is divination by earth, since *geo* means earth, and *mancia* is divination. Like astronomy, this art makes a display of using a system of houses. In this art one first makes four figures, and from the last four figures one makes two witnesses, and from the witnesses one makes a judge. From these figures, the masters of the art think they can inquire and gain knowledge of all things, future and past.

Chapter 39: The great labor and skill required for geomancy

This art requires much skill, for just as in astronomy, so, too, here one must distinguish every variety of appearance and conjunction. Albert the Great says that among all the forbidden arts none is more legitimate than the art of geomancy.[44] Yet your princely grace should know that this art is a sin and forbidden, and has no foundation whatsoever. I can prove that in this way: let two or three great masters in the art weigh a question, which of two lords will win a combat, and you will notice that one of them does not answer like the other. Further, let one master answer the same question twice, and he will not reach the same conclusion. Further still, the art has no foundation other than marking points, even or odd, which come out by casting of lots.[45] That and all other casting of lots is forbidden by holy Scripture and by the section [of canon law] devoted to sorcery.[46] Further, what power do the figures have, or what are they supposed to mean? Those who set out to make them already have in mind [the answers to] the questions they want to know about, and they think the heavenly forces determine the outcome. But that is pure trumpery, since in all the art of stargazing the masters can inquire and learn about nothing more than

44. Zambelli, *The "Speculum astronomiae"*, 273, where geomancy has at least qualified approval on account of its scientific grounding (it is based on the "ratio" or "reason" of number) and the favor of many but unspecified authorities.

45. JH-1989, 147.

46. *Decretum*, pt. 2, causa 26, qu. 5, chaps. 1–11, given in *CIC*, vol. 1, cols. 1027–33.

is purely natural, as Your Grace will hear explained later on. For how can the stars give what they themselves do not possess?

Chapter 39a: How the art of geomancy operates

I will explain to your princely grace what takes place in the art. When the master of this art despairs of his natural art and senses, he falls into superstition and thinks he can investigate what he wants to know by means of lots. That is a grievous offense against God, for if we cannot obtain something with our senses and reason we should appeal only to the Lord God, who can and will teach our reason and our sense, and none other. But if the master is so mad in his senses and so beclouded in his reason that he seeks counsel other than from God, then on account of his unbelief God allows the evil Devil to become involved in the casting of lots and making of figures. And when the master has made the figures and applies his wits to that exercise, then the Devil is promptly at hand, suggesting to him the answer to his question, and often he comes back all at once with the truth. He does that in order to deceive all the more deeply the master and all who believe in him, and to lead them into eternal damnation. Thus the almighty God allows the sin and the sinner to be punished and tormented on this account.

Chapter 40: A lesson in how great a sin it is to engage in the forbidden arts

O most esteemed prince, you must know in your deep reason and understanding how great a sin it is for a person to forget God and to seek help, guidance, and counsel in the devilish arts. God expressly forbade this in the fifth book of Moses, called Deuteronomy, where he says, "Take heed, O Israel, that you do not pursue the unbelief of the heathen! And there should be none among you who consults a fortune-teller or an interpreter of dreams. There should also not be among you a conjurer or sorcerer, and none should seek counsel from the false fortune-tellers or seek to know future things. Further, none of you should inquire about the truth from the dead, for God hates all these things deeply. On account of such unbelief God will forbid entry into the promised land, because the pagans have and pursue such unbelief, sorcery, and fortune-telling. But you, Israel, are taught differently about true things."[47]

Chapter 41: How God alone gives right prophecy

God has said, he will raise up a true prophet out of your lineage and people.[48] It is from him you should seek answers, and he is the one you should follow. Now all the teachers say that Jesus Christ, the true Son of God, is that very prophet, whose counsel one should seek and follow. The teachers say further that a righteous person, without sin, may merit to obtain from God whatever he will, even knowledge of all future and past things, as the prophets of old did, and also the dear saints; these [saints] pursued the true art, compelling and adjuring the Devil with true power, as Paul compelled the Devil to work; Saint Margaret, Saint Juliana, and other women have forced and compelled the Devil only with the help of God.[49] So also may a true Christian man force and compel the devils with his pious prayer. Thus, O highborn prince, you should believe that nothing can compel the Devil except a pure mind of a blessed person, and only with the power of God.

Chapter 42: Whether casting lots is permissible

It is a serious question, whether it is permissible to cast lots, as is often done regarding land and people, often also regarding inheritance and

---

47. The quotation from Deuteronomy 18:9–14 is loose, and Hartlieb erroneously gives chapter 23 as the location.

48. Cf. Deuteronomy 18:15, 18:18; Acts 3:22, 7:37.

49. Jacobus de Voragine, *The Golden Legend: Readings on the Saints*, trans. William Granger Ryan, 2 vols. (Princeton, NJ: Princeton University Press, 1993), 1:160–61 (for the story of Juliana); 2:233 (that of Margaret); and either 1:355 or 2:239 (for that of Paul).

property, and wine and other merchandise, as merchants do in ordinary transactions, casting lots to decide who gets this or that portion. The teachers of holy Scripture answer that there are many forms of casting lots, as when it is done over inheritance and property and merchandise, that are not sinful but allowed. But when casting lots is done to investigate secret things, such as theft, to determine which person has stolen goods, or when a person wants to cast lots to determine if a spouse has broken marital fidelity, doing it in these and similar matters is forbidden and decidedly a sin. And the doctors believe this because the evil Devil involves himself in all situations of doubt, and whenever there is fickleness and instability of people's senses, and in all these cases he incites, aids, and guides toward evil. And whenever he is able to bring innocent people into calumny and suspicion, he eagerly does so; and people commit sin in these matters.

Chapter 43: About cases where casting of lots falls out once or twice the same way

Even when casting lots comes out the same way a first time and a second, and thus makes an assured prediction, still one should not believe in it, since the Devil brings that about only so as to bring people over all the more strongly to such superstition and sorcery. You should also know, most gracious lord, that God will not tolerate any suspicion between [himself and] his spouse, that is the soul. He wants people to honor and love him alone, and in all needs to call only on him, and not on his handiwork and creatures. Your Grace should mark well, for this point will often be raised when I come to discuss the minor arts.

Chapter 44: About the books of lots

There is a commonly known type of book called a lot book that sometimes involves casting dice, sometimes reckoning a number so that after finding the number one seeks the answer to a question that a person wants answered, whether about women, livestock, gaining of honors or offices, or various other things, whether a sick person will die or get well, whether one will fall into hardship, whether a person will have good or bad fortune in this or that affair. The wickedness is so wide-ranging in these questions that there is nothing in the world that cannot be found in these interrogations. In these operations one comes to an Old Man, who refers the questioner to a Judge, who answers the question that has been posed. All this is superstition and is very much contrary to God, for it has no foundation, neither spiritual nor natural, and is strictly forbidden by Holy Church in canon law.[50] Your Grace and every Christian person should avoid and flee from these books of lots.

Chapter 45: That excuses do not help to justify unbelief

Perhaps your princely grace or someone else might say, "I place no faith in such arts, I pursue them only for entertainment." O dear prince, just think about what might happen! A simple person might be standing by who perhaps holds and believes that such things are true, and what the princes do their subjects take as done rightly. Such a person's soul would then be eternally lost. Take heed, my dearest lord, what great loss ensues from such a small thing. A soul is better and nobler than all the world and all earthly goods, but it is lost on account of some minor unbelief. Take heed, what happens in the case of great offenses, in which God is denied, sacrifice is made to the Devil, and a person submits himself to the evil Devil. On that account an entire city could rightly perish. Dear prince, do not allow any such thing in your lands, and God will reward you a thousandfold.

Chapter 46: How the holy apostles cast lots

Your Grace might also say, "The holy Apostles cast lots for [the election of] Matthias [Acts 1:26], so why should I too not cast lots?" The

50. Peters, *The Magician, the Witch, and the Law*, 98–102.

teachers of holy Scripture say in this regard that where one is seeking to further God's honor and praise, one may cast lots with fear of God. Thus, if you had two priests of good character and learning who were asking you for a parish, then Your Grace could cast lots about which of them would be better for the common folk, and that casting of lots would not be a sin. The dear Apostles acted in this way. Further, Your Grace should know that some things in the Old Testament and at the beginning of Christian Church were not sins, but Holy Church has forbidden them, and we should and must obey the holy Church if we wish to be saved.

Chapter 47: Casting lots to see who will win or lose a [single] combat

Certain sorcerers would like to know who will win a [single] combat. They write the two names on two slips of paper, and cover them with paste or wax, then place them in a bowl filled with water. That is a great unbelief and serious sin, and forbidden, because someone might draw comfort from this fraud who has never before engaged in sword fighting, and he may win or not win, since this art is all trumpery.

Chapter 48: Another cunning and sinful ploy involving the casting of lots

There is another common, cunning ploy that the evil devils and their associates have thought up to determine who will win at jousting, racing, or fencing. The procedure is, alas, quite sinful, for it involves much reference to the pure, chaste Virgin Mary, in whom there was never any unbelief or suspicion or doubt in matters of Christian belief, for when all the light [of faith] was extinguished in all the Apostles, hers burned all the brighter.[51] The pure mother of God cannot endure

---

51. Albert the Great was known for promoting this belief; see Maria Burger, "Albert the Great—Mariology," in *A Companion to Albert the Great: Theology, Philosophy, and the Sciences*, ed. Irven M. Resnick (Leiden: Brill, 2013),

129. The theme occurs in the *Malleus maleficarum*, pt. 1, qu. 6; see Christopher S. Mackay, trans., *The Hammer of Witches: A Complete Translation of the "Malleus maleficarum"* (Cambridge, UK: Cambridge University Press, 2009).

being mixed up in these false, evil unbeliefs. The holy knight Saint George, too, who endured great torments for the sake of God and Christian faith, is not spared, but is also mixed up in these evil sorceries and unbeliefs.[52] For the masters of this art say that certain epithets pertain to the pure maiden Mary and certain days of the week belong to Our Lady, such as Saturday, Tuesday, and Thursday, while the rest of the days belong to Saint George. On this basis they determine who will conquer. It is really a great pity that the names of the pure, chaste maiden Mary and the holy Christian knight Saint George are used in such evil, vile unbeliefs.

Chapter 49: About the books of lots by Pythagoras

There are other books having to do with such calculation, such as the books of Pythagoras, who gives many letters and figures, and for each letter there are certain numbers; by means of these one determines who will win, which is surely a superstition. Further, one of these books, also ascribed to Pythagoras, teaches which of two spouses will die sooner.[53] The same book has caused frequent and serious conflict between married couples, which is the source of great pity and lament. Esteemed prince, you should not allow that in your princedom when Your Grace encounters it. For according to holy Scripture, each person should prevent such sin as he can prevent, and one who does not do so is guilty of that sin. That is what the teacher to Datus writes.[54]

Chapter 50: What a sin it is when one uses sorcery on account of theft

There is another superstition: When someone has incurred loss, there are people who conjure a loaf of bread and stick three knives into it, making three crosses, and attach a spindle and a spindle whorl to it,

52. *HDA*, vol. 1, cols. 647–57.

53. See John D. Mikalson, *Greek Popular Religion in Greek Philosophy* (Oxford, UK: Oxford University Press, 2010), 111–12.

54. The source eludes Ulm and also Eisermann and Graf, and remains unobvious. Possibly a garbled reference to Ecclesiastes ("The Teacher") 2:26, 9:18, or 10:4?

and two persons hold it on their ring fingers,[55] and they conjure by the holy Apostles. This is a great sin, because often an innocent person falls under suspicion, which hangs over him unresolved until his death. You are guilty of that, you master! Take heed to atone for that,[56] for you must suffer forever unless you remove the suspicion from such a person. Oh, how difficult that is! There are more people who exercise this lot casting and test God, using a psalter with a stole wrapped around it. That is a twofold superstition, because using holy and consecrated things for sin and against the commandment of Holy Church is a terrible heresy and an evil superstition.

Chapter 51: About the blessing of cheese

One finds people who bless a piece of cheese and believe that the person guilty of theft cannot eat any of that cheese. Although soap is sometimes given in place of cheese, still it is a sin, for it quite often happens that great slander and evil suspicion arise from it. You should guard yourself from this practice. The things of this sort are so many and so countless that no one could describe them all. Yet it is the definitive judgment and opinion of holy Scripture that no one should investigate future things or secret things with lot casting of any sort, for God is the true knower of all things, and one should honor him and call on him with pure, sincere prayer, because he reveals to his dear chosen ones what they seek after. Further, the evil Devil, the archenemy of humankind, involves himself in all such lot casting and forbidden arts, and by them he leads poor people astray.

Chapter 52: Why sorcery sometimes fails and sometimes does not fail

You may say, "How does it happen that such arts sometimes come out right and sometimes do not?" In this regard you should know that in

55. *uf den ungenanten vinger*: see *HDA*, vol. 2, col. 1495.

56. Eisermann and Graf note this as a problematic passage and deal with it differently.

such matters the Devil sometimes delays, so that you will render him more and greater honor and he can bind you all the more and more deeply in his service. For whatever the Devil does or lets be done, he lays snares and deceptions for people, so as to draw poor frivolous people more and more to himself. Your princely grace should be on guard against that, and against all casting of lots, for some people sin in this way unwittingly, and do not believe it is a sin. Let this section serve as counsel for Your Grace about the art of geomancy.

G. CORRELATION OF ARTS WITH ELEMENTS

Chapter 53: How these four forbidden arts are named for the four elements

Your princely grace should note well that the four arts—geomancy, hydromancy, aeromancy, and pyromancy—are named for the four elements. For just as geomancy is divination by the earth, so hydromancy is divination by water, and aeromancy is divination by the air, and pyromancy is divination by fire. Note well, highborn prince, how the four elements are poisoned with the evil Devil's tricks and specters, so that, alas, many people among the pagans and Christians are damned thereby. Alas and alack, no one is so deeply guilty of this as the frivolous princes who have no proper, true faith in God. One wants to dig for treasure, another wants to inquire into the secrets of another prince, another wants to become victorious by the Devil's art, another wants to use sorcery to court favor or to sow love and hatred. In truth this is all trumpery and seriously contrary to God. O, my dearest lord and brother-in-law, who can believe that the great enemy of all men, the Devil, can ever do anything good? Indeed no, he may show you things sweeter than honey, but his purpose is in truth more bitter than poisonous gall. Yes, most gracious prince, have you or anyone ever heard that any person has ever obtained anything good in body or possessions from the Devil? But that much harm has come to many persons—kings, princes, great bishops—from the Devil, on that point I could write for you a long history. But that is not necessary, because I do not doubt that Your Grace knows that yourself.

H. HYDROMANCY

Chapter 54: About the third forbidden art, called hydromancy

Now I will describe the third art, forbidden by God and by Holy Church, hydromancy, which involves the use of water.[57] The masters of this art have a fundamental principle which is a great error in faith, for they say that God did not create water, and they claim as basis the first book of the Bible, in the story of creation. It is written there how the spirit of the Lord hovers over the water [Genesis 1:2], and they believe there are special spirits which live in the water, and which reveal all future and past things; and the greatest and most powerful among all these spirits they call Salathiel,[58] and when they want to carry out their art they make offering to that spirit with burning of candles, and this is a form of superstition, the greatest and most serious.

Chapter 55: How the art of hydromancy takes place

When the master of this art wants to investigate a theft, or seek for treasure, or learn about something else secret, he goes on Sunday before sunrise to three flowing springs and takes a little from each in a pure polished glass, and carries it home to a finely arranged chamber. Then he burns candles before it, and he gives honor to the water as if to God himself. This is surely a great sin, heresy, and superstition. Afterward he takes a pure child and sets him on a fine chair in front of the water.[59] Oh, how happy the evil Devil is, when someone does him such service with pure children! O you proud Belial, you who know well that you fell on account of your pride from the eternal heavenly throne, and you still do not desist from your pride! You are eager to mislead pure children, too, and you think it

---

57. *HDA*, vol. 4, cols. 548–74.

58. Gustav Davidson, *A Dictionary of Angels, Including the Fallen Angels* (New York: Free Press, 1967), 254.

59. See Kieckhefer, *Forbidden Rites*, 98, 100, 104, 120–21.

redounds to your praise when these pure children pay you the divine veneration that belongs only to God. Surely your misfortune only becomes greater.

Chapter 56: What the child does in the art of hydromancy

When the pure child sits there, the master of sorcery stands behind him and speaks certain unknown words into his ear. Then he reads some unknown words and bids the pure child repeat those words. What the words signify, neither I nor any master can explain, other than that a person alienates himself from God with such mysterious words and gives himself to the evil Devil. O Lord God, have mercy on the innocent pure child! Trust me, O most esteemed prince, that I have seen a great deal of these dealings, and I have observed that when these words are used the children suffer grievous harm thereby.[60] Truly, O lord, there is no truth in this art, and it is always a pity that priests do not more vigorously forbid and fight against this superstition and sorcery with the aid and support of the princes.

Chapter 57: How the master interrogates the boy

When the master has the boy before him, he bids him tell what he sees, then he inquires about treasure, theft, or something else, as he wishes. The simplicity of the child brings it about that he says he saw this or that; the evil Devil then involves himself in this, and often lets falsehood appear for truth. He does this only to mislead people all the more and bring them into evil suspicion, causing one person to sin along with another. For all the work, help, and counsel of the Devil end up misleading people and bringing them into superstition, in which they deny their God.

---

60. See the comments of John of Salisbury, *Policraticus*, bk. 2, chap. 28, sec. 165, in *Frivolities of Courtiers and Footprints of Philosophers*, trans. Joseph B. Pike (Minneapolis: University of Minnesota Press, 1938), 147.

Chapter 58: How one takes water for the art of hydromancy

There are quite a few ways one can take water, for some draw it from running waterways, letting it flow into a glass; others take it from still pools and always boil it in honor of the spirits who in their opinion have power over the water; the lord and prince of them all is Salathiel, as the masters declare. But it is a superstition, for God alone is lord over water and all things, for he made them out of nothing, which the Devil cannot do. The Devil may indeed create an illusion, when God permits him that on account of our sin and superstition, but in fact he cannot create anew the smallest thing that ever was. He also cannot transform one thing essentially into another, but only in seeming and appearance. Oh, how often and how much a pious person is brought into suspicion and slander through such arts, and all in vain, only on the basis of the evil Devil's trickery! O you masters, you must atone for all that or else be eternally lost. These are the words of holy Scripture: "Sin is not forgiven, unless you give back what you have taken."[61] Oh, how can you give back someone's reputation? Take heed!

Chapter 59: How hydromancy is carried out even with holy water

It does not suffice the evil Devil that he misleads people with the mere element of water—he does so also with holy water. For there are unfortunately quite a few people who carry out great sorcery and superstition with holy water, which is consecrated only to wash away our venial sins. Many people abuse it for superstition and sorcery. There are scarcely any forms of sorcery for which the masters and old women do not use holy water; likewise many people give holy water to their cattle to drink, thinking wolves cannot eat or harm them then. This is superstition, since the water is consecrated for people and not for cattle.

---

61. Presumably a reference to Ezekiel 33:15, but see also Exodus 22:1, Leviticus 6:4–5, Ezekiel 18:7–16 and 20:11, and Luke 19:8.

Chapter 60: How old women sprinkle their herbs for [protection against] worms

Some women sprinkle their herbs and plants with it, and they think caterpillars will then not attack them. That is a superstition that you, the bishops, the pastors, and other priests should uproot. There are many courtiers who, when they have new spurs, will dunk them along with their wheels into a holy water stoop, and they claim that what they hit with these [i.e., what part of a horse's body] will never again swell up.[62] All that is superstition. Many sorceresses go to a mill wheel and catch the water that sprays into the air from the wheel; with that water they carry out many forms of sorcery for love and for enmity. And if someone is unable to be a proper man [i.e., is impotent], they use it to help him be a proper man. All that is superstition. Many people mix other things into the water and use it to carry out all sorts of sorcery, making a person unable to do something, or the like. That is a great superstition and a deception of the Devil.

Chapter 61: How sorcery is carried out with many [forms of] water

There are many evil Christians who carry out sorcery with various forms of water, such as the blessed, consecrated [water of] baptism, on which the salvation and blessedness of all Christians depends; they perform sorcery with it and do a great deal with it that should not be written down. Indeed, when old women get ahold of the [water of] baptism, they think they have "won the cock."[63] I will leave out what could be written about that, even though I know that your princely grace is so endowed by God with high reason and wisdom that Your Grace would not be led into trouble by it, but would be strengthened all the more in all Christian works. Yet I am concerned that this book

---

62. The material in brackets follows the translation of Eisermann and Graf.

63. *den haan ertantzt*, meaning they won a rooster by dancing; see *HDA*, vol. 3, cols. 1345–46.

might come into hands of the imprudent people, who would indeed
be led into trouble.

Chapter 62: How many sorcerers cast lead into water and carry out sorcery in that way

Likewise there are many masters in the art of hydromancy who carry
out their trickery with water in which they have cast hot lead or tin,
and they note precisely how much bubbling and how much froth
comes up in the water; they carry out their superstition and their
tricks of sorcery in this way, and they perform their fortune-telling
with it. When they gaze at the water, it is called hydromancy, but when
they gaze at the lead or tin for their fortune-telling then the art is
called pyromancy, which I will write about after this art.

Chapter 63: How sorcery is carried out with floating [objects]

Another trick of sorcery is carried out with water: some people take
two things, such as wooden sticks, or straws, or light coins, for example a halfpenny, and they designate one for one person, the other for
another person; and when the two things float together on the water
in a bowl then the two [persons] are going to come together; but if
one flows away from the other, then they are not going to come
together; and the one that flows away fastest will be the guilty party.
The masters of this superstition also try to determine which of two
married persons will die sooner, for they believe that whichever
[object] sinks first, that [person] will die first.

Chapter 64: How sorcery is carried out for [single] combat

They do such things also in the case of [single] combat, as I have said
previously with regard to casting lots. All that is a great superstition,
and the greatest [offense] in it is that people do it by preference on
holy nights when they should be serving God. They carry out this

superstition, for instance, on the eve of Saint Thomas, on the three nights before Pentecost,[64] before Christmas eve, on Christmas itself, and on the other nights of the Christmas season. In many lands that is so common that young and old people alike think it is no sin. But that is not the case, because it is a superstition that the pagans engaged in many years ago and still engage in; and it is forbidden by Holy Church.

Chapter 65: About the water of Saint Blaise

Likewise water is blessed on Saint Blaise Day, which is used for purposes other than those prescribed by the Church.[65] Whoever does that engages in superstition, and it is always a mortal sin. There are also many people who bless water and heal wounds with it, and think after that the wounds cannot swell. That is all pure superstition, for the blessing gives the water no power besides what the holy Church has established. Making other types of water with herbs, roots, and other such things no doubt means such types of water have power— that of the things with which they are made—but all that is natural, and does not involve blessings or words. In the same way, eye doctors make water for the eyes that is quite good. But one should not make these types of water on particular days, as if they had more power on one day than on others. This is a superstition, and whoever does such things is always committing mortal sin.

Chapter 66: How sorcery is used in digging up herbs

Something of the sort [i.e., observation of particular times] is used also in digging for herbs: doing that is always a superstition and a mortal sin. A person who is clever enough to dig for a particular herb in its month does well. One can also dig for herbs, or cut wood and the like, under a full moon or when the moon is waning. All that is

---

64. *HDA*, vol. 6, cols. 1684–94.   65. JH-1989, 140; *HDA*, vol. 1, cols. 1360–65.

not a sin, because it takes place naturally. You should also note that many kinds of lot casting and superstition are carried out with water, but I have left that out for the sake of brevity.

I. AEROMANCY

Chapter 67: About the fourth art, called aeromancy

Now I will write about the fourth art, which is forbidden and is called aeromancy.[66] It involves use of the air, and the things that hover and live in it. The art is very common among the pagans; they have such great superstition of this sort that they worship and venerate what appears to them first [in the morning], and they venerate it that day as their god. Evil Christians carry out much superstition with this art, for they say that when someone encounters a hare that is bad luck, while if someone encounters a wolf that is great good luck. There are many sorts of this superstition, involving many animals. There are people who believe that if the birds fly at someone's right hand that means great advantage and great luck, while if they fly at a person's left hand that means bad luck and loss. All that is superstition. There are people who have great faith in the eagle and believe that if it flies to their right that means great good luck or great advantage.

Chapter 68: Further reproof of the evil art

There are people who have such great faith in this that they hang their carrying satchel on the other side if the eagle changes its direction, as often incidentally happens. They have great faith in such things, and they believe it is unfailing. But does the Devil involve himself in this art, too, in order to misguide and mislead people? Indeed, without doubt, the Devil is the true founder and inciter of this art! He even changes himself into these birds in order to deceive people. Every

66. *HDA*, vol. 1, cols. 203–6.

Christian should be on guard against such things, because they are very much contrary to God.

Chapter 69: How many people go hawking and hunting on specific days, which is a great superstition

There are also many princes, rich and poor lords, who do their hunting on certain days, and when this or that wind is blowing. All that is superstition. But the masters of the hunt know well that they should take their direction from the wind, and their use of hounds is according to the wind, and that is not a sin, since it is natural and is the highest art of the hunters. Many people wear tall feathers in their hats; they do this so they will know from where the wind comes, and they believe that in many matters they have their fortune against the wind while in others they have their fortune with the wind. All that is superstition and sorcery, and no one should believe in that. The fortune of a pious man is to be found in all places throughout the world.

Chapter 70: How people engage in sorcery and carry out superstition with feathers

This superstition is now so common that courtiers, even women and maidens, wear feathers without knowing why. And although it is unwitting, the evil Devil takes satisfaction in it and misleads many of his followers thereby,[67] allowing the masters of this art to carry out their art all the more without notice. Your princely grace should not permit all that or anything else connected with superstition; and if you take the lead, as the wisest and oldest prince in all the German lands, then the younger ones will act according to your governance. Thus you will gain reward and grace from God and great honor and esteem from all the world.

---

67. *und verlait vil seiner menschen damit*, which Eisermann and Graf note as problematic and suggest might better be *reiner menschen*. This would suggest the Devil misleads many who have been upright—a possible reading.

Chapter 71: A good example concerning Roland

One reads in the history of Charles the Great how Roland, Oliver, and Bishop Turpin remained in Galicia while Charles withdrew, and the wind came up and helped Roland get through the enemy; and his horn set the air in motion when he blew it.[68] Your princely grace should believe me, that the fortune-tellers put much faith in this and place the foundation of the art in particular on this short statement: "The wind came up and helped Roland through the enemy." Now your princely grace knows well that Charles the Grace, Roland, and other godly Christians, bishops and princes, all set out in the service of Jesus Christ and wished for nothing other than his grace. How then could they have practiced superstition or sorcery? Everything they did and had done they placed in God's power, as we Christians should all do. Truly, they never resorted to superstition, for the true God was with them at all times, as is quite evident on the graves at the last battle in Roncesvalles.

Chapter 72: An example showing that one should be on guard against the Devil

You should take note and realize, O virtuous prince, how the Devil seeks out and contrives so many tricks with which he misleads people into superstition and his trumpery. He has suggested to his masters that the holy warriors of God, such as Charles and Roland, also believed in the evil, wicked, forbidden arts, so that poor men are misguided and misled thereby.

68. Kevin R. Poole, ed. and trans., *The Chronicle of Pseudo-Turpin: Book IV of the "Liber Sancti Jacobi (Codex Calixtinus)"* (New York: Italica, 2014), 64–65. See Adriana Kremenjas-Danicic, ed., *Roland's European Paths* (Dubrovnik: Europski dom Dubrovnik, 2006); Rita Lejeune and Jacques Stiennon, *The Legend of Roland in the Mid-* dle Ages (New York: Phaidon, 1971); and especially (for the significance of Roland in late medieval German lands) Achim Timmermann, "'Freedom I do reveal to you': Scale, Microarchitecture, and the Rise of the Turriform Civic Monument in Fourteenth-Century Northern Europe," *Art History* 38 (2015): 337–39.

Chapter 73: How people have superstitions with regard to sneezing

There is another superstition in this art, and that is this: when a person sneezes, thus naturally purging the brain, they take it for a great sign of fortune or unfortune, and they use it for fortune-telling. If there are three sneezes, then there are four thieves about the house. If there are two, the person should get up and lie somewhere else to sleep. If there are thirteen, that is supposed to be very good, and whatever appears in the night [in dreams] is supposed to be turned to good. But in the morning, when the person rises from bed, the sneezes have different meaning. There are many such things, and it is all pure superstition, for all the masters of medicine know why it is that a person sneezes: sneezing comes from warm air that collects in the head and comes out powerfully through narrow openings. For that reason it makes a loud noise, as Hippocrates said in the sixth book of his *Aphorisms*.[69] All that is natural, and signifies neither fortune nor unfortune in other matters, for the head purges and cleans itself in the process.

Chapter 74: What sneezing is

Many masters of natural medicine say that such sneezing comes close to a stroke, for if the strong winds are stopped up in the brain and do not come out, then before long the person will have a stroke; and for that reason some masters refer to the lesser apoplexy, which is to say a small stroke. For when a person sneezes, he has no control over his members, but by the grace of God it does not last long, and so it comes out for the best.

Chapter 75: About comets and signs in the heavens

At times there appear in the sky many wondrous signs, stars that the common people call dragons, but the art of astronomy calls these

---

69. Hippocrates, *The Aphorisms of Hippocrates*, trans. Thomas Coar (1822; repr., Birmingham, AL: Classics of Medicine Library, 1982), sect. 6, no. 13, p. 164: *A singultu detento sternutationes supervenientes, solvunt singultum* ("Sneezing suspends hiccough"). See JH-1914, lxv; JH-1989, 144–45.

signs comets. They can appear in two figures and forms, many of
which Ptolemy described, as did Albumasar.[70] But their meaning is
only natural, and they signify natural influence that occurs by natural
cause. Exercising the art [of interpreting them] belongs to the proper
stargazers, and when they explain these signs according to their
natural courses, it is not a sin or forbidden. But when others wish to
involve themselves in it, then the Devil's trumpery plays a role. Yet
you must proceed circumspectly, wisely, and with careful attention,
you stargazers! I, Doctor Hartlieb, give you this counsel, for I know
of great masters who in these affairs have been caught up in deep
scandal.

Chapter 76: How the physicians also write about such signs

The wise physicians also write about some such signs, such as Avicenna in his first book on the transformation and change of the air,
and they call these signs *azub*, and say that they usually denote death
and pestilence.[71] The physicians may also predict future things from
these signs, insofar as they have natural causes. But if a physician
speaks more about this than he can discern from natural causes, then
he surely falls into error, and I fear what he says is not without suggestion and deceit of the Devil. Your princely grace should be on guard
against this.

Chapter 77: How sorcerers using the art of aeromancy interpret the signs in the sky but not following natural principles

The masters in the art of aeromancy do not consider the signs in the
sky in this way, but they believe such signs refer in particular to future

70. On Ptolemy see *HMES*, vol. 1,
pp. 104–16.
71. *Flores Avicenne collecti super
quinque canonibus*, ed. Michael de

Capella (Lyon: Gilbert de Villiers, 1514),
fols. 11ʳ–12ᵛ.

things and other such matters, and so they inquire and desire to know in secret. In this they deceive themselves, and also other people, for, to put it bluntly, there is no foundation or truth in this art. There are also many people, especially great princes, who firmly think and believe that when great storms come this means there will be great treason. That is a great error, for if one wishes to know why great winds come about he should read the book of Aristotle called *Meteorology*; he will find all the causes of winds, and there is nothing written there about treason.[72] Whoever believes such things falls into superstition, for the elements cannot have effect on human free will.[73] Therefore, O esteemed prince, put no credence in these things. Treason comes about from personal free evil will, and no one is compelled to engage in it, rather the evil Devil incites people to it; but whoever wishes can resist him.

Chapter 78: How some engage in sorcery with birds

There are some sorcerers who kill birds and then cast their blood into the air, saying there are particular spirits in the air, to whom they make sacrifice, and they believe they can appease these spirits and bring it about that they serve them and reveal secret and hidden things. All that is superstition and a misleading of humankind, for wherever the Devil goes,[74] his evil and deceit follow him about. We often hear and read how certain people can fly in the air; I have written about that above, since that theme belongs more to the art of nigramancy than to that of aeromancy.

72. Aristotle, *Meteorologica*, bk. 2, chaps. 4–6, 359b–365a, trans. E. W. Webster (Oxford, UK: Clarendon, 1923); *The Complete Works of Aristotle*, rev. ed., trans. Jonathan Barnes (Princeton, NJ: Princeton University Press, 2014), 3310–12.

73. Theodore Otto Wedel, *The Mediaeval Attitude Toward Astrology, Particularly in England* (New Haven, CT: Yale University Press, 1920), 60–89.

74. *wann der tewffel sey wär*: here my reading basically follows Eisermann and Graf's.

Chapter 79: How many people make use of figures and images in carrying out sorcery

There are also many sorceresses who make images and figures of wax and other material.[75] They make these at various times, pronouncing many known and unknown names, then they hang them up in the air. And as the wind blows it about, they think the man in whose name it is made will have no rest. All that is great superstition and sorcery. Many do that with an aspen leaf, writing on it their sorcery, and thinking they can thus bring about love between people.

Chapter 79a: Chapter about magic images

I have read much about such images in the art of magic, which is a mixture of lore about the stars, and certain unknown words, and other strange things. All that is true sorcery and an evil superstition. I have also heard a great deal said about how women make such images and heat them by a fire so as to torment men. That is without doubt a great superstition and cannot work without the Devil's special help. O prince, there are many such people in the German lands! If Your Princely Grace undertakes to punish them Your Grace will find many to help and support you. But unfortunately no one will undertake this, since such evil, contemptible, superstitious people are mostly protected by the princes. O Jesus, have mercy on these poor misguided people, and raise up a properly faithful prince to hate and help exterminate such sorcery. There is much of this sorcery, with which women think they can cause love or pain, and I will write about that separately when I have finished writing on the seven main forbidden arts.

J. PYROMANCY

Chapter 80: About the forbidden art called pyromancy

Now I will speak and write about the fifth art of sorcery and superstition, which in Latin is called *pyromancia*.[76] May God grant that I carry

75. *atzman.*　　　　　76. *HDA*, vol. 7, cols. 400–414.

this out well, for many people are misguided and misled by this art and fall into great superstition. The art is called pyromancy, meaning divination by fire. As the Devil carries out his trickery to mislead people with other elements, so he does also with fire. There are women and men who take it upon themselves to make fire, and then in that fire they see past and future things. The masters and mistresses of this devilish art have particular days on which they have wood prepared, and when they want to carry out their art they go to a secret place and take with them poor, foolish people, whose fortunes they mean to tell. They have them kneel down and make sacrifice to the angel of fire, whom they honor and venerate. Along with this offering, they kindle the wood, and the master looks directly into the fire, and he observes carefully what appears to him in it.[77]

Chapter 81: How this art operates

Many people say they see things in the fire as in a mirror; they are counted as true masters and mistresses. The Devil takes great pains to deceive them in this way. Some of them examine the fire and its flames to see if it burns straight upward without deviation. They then declare accordingly how their affairs will proceed. Some take note how the smoke rises, whether crooked or straight, and that is their art, and they make grand statements according to whether the fire burns bright or dark; and that is the best grounding [they have for the art]. O dear God, what meager foundation this art has! Truly no other foundation than that the evil Devil deceives and misleads frivolous people, for in actuality if the wood is green it gives thick and watery smoke, if it is dry and thin it gives light and lovely flame, if it is windy the smoke bends over, while if it is misty the flame turns sideways and can not rise straight up. Take note, most esteemed prince, how the poor people are misled. Take action against this sin, my lord—the time has surely come.

77. Eisermann and Graf note that this is a problematic passage; my reading is a bit less interpretive than theirs is.

Chapter 82: Another error in the art

We find masters of this art who take fat from various animals, which out of caution I will not name. They burn it and think they see many things in the smoke, which is all trickery of the Devil. Some of the masters and disciples in this art of pyromancy take entire entrails and burn them on the Devil's altar, then prophesy from the appearance of the smoke, and this superstition has a special name, which is *auspicium*.

Chapter 83: How people carry out the art of pyromancy

People exercise the art of pyromancy in many ways and forms. Some masters of the art take a pure child and seat him in their laps, and raise their hand up and have [the child] look at his nail, and they conjure the child and the nail with a great conjuration, then they speak three unknown words in the child's ear. One of them is "Oriel";[78] on the others I remain silent, out of caution. Then they ask the child whatever they want, and they think the child should see it in the nail. All that is pure superstition, and you, O Christian, should be on guard against it.

Chapter 84: Another great error in the faith committed with pyromancy

There is a further element of deceptive trumpery in the art, when the masters take oil and grime from a pan and anoint a pure child's hand, either girl or boy, making it shine brightly, then raise the hand up to the sun so that the sun shines in it, or they hold candles up to the hand and have the child look at it, then they ask the child whatever they want. According to them, whatever the child says will turn out true. Unfortunately they do not know how the evil Devil involves himself

---

78. Davidson, *A Dictionary of Angels*, 215.

in this and has much more error than truth appear. He does that so that frivolous people will be misguided and misled into eternal damnation. The masters also speak unknown words into the child's ears. It is greatly to be feared that by means of such unknown words people unwittingly court damnation, for those who make vows to the evil spirits and pacts with the Devil must always deny God.

Chapter 85: A lesson and a good counsel on how one should be on guard against unknown words

O virtuous and enlightened prince, be on guard against such unknown words, for who knows what they signify! One of these words is "Ragel."[79] I have taken great pains in my time to learn the meaning of such words, and I have asked many people, including Jews, but they did not know these words. I have asked Greeks, Tartars, Turks, their physicians and stargazers. I have also asked Jewesses, but still I have not found out what the words mean. In my opinion there is reason for concern that these words form association and pact with the devils, as I have mentioned several times already.

Chapter 86: How this art is done with a steel mirror

The art of pyromancy is also carried out with a steel mirror, around which many characters and strange figures are engraved.[80] One also whispers secret words secretly into the ears of a child, and asks him then whatever one wishes, and the master believes the child will see everything. All that is trumpery. I have seen masters who say they prepare a mirror so that any person, woman or man, can see whatever he wishes. Take note of a trickery of the evil Devil: these people always confess their sins in advance, but they dare not confess the sin that is greatest of all, since it is true idolatry, sorcery, and superstition. Notice

---

79. Ibid., 238, under "Raguel."

80. Kieckhefer, *Forbidden Rites*, 98–100, 104–6; *HDA*, vol. 4, cols. 1099–1107.

how the Devil and the master of this art lead and misguide poor people into eternal damnation. The art often fails the masters, and the Devil does that so that he will obtain even greater services and sacrifices from the frivolous people. The same frivolous people and their masters say that this and other such arts involve good angels, and they say, "Well, one must confess and be pure, so how could this be a sin?"

Chapter 87: How people commit great sin by prayer and fasting

O Christian, you should believe me: you may confess, fast, pray, attend services, and the like, all of which is seemingly good, but when you do otherwise than holy Church has allowed and established, it is all a mortal sin for you, for you engage in superstition in the process, and it may well be that you do not confess and fast in the way the Christian Church commands. Oh, cry to God, that many people are so quick to do the Devil's service but so slow in God's service! Truly, the one a person serves is the one who will reward him. This art and this exercise in particular is a very great superstition.

Chapter 88: Another way the art is carried out

The masters and those like them exercise this art also with a smooth mirror, and have children look in it, conjuring them and whispering secret words to them, and they believe they can learn a great deal by doing so. That is all a superstition and a trickery and temptation of the evil Devil. Guard yourself, you Christian, I earnestly warn you! They also use for this purpose a fine sword, polished to a shine. And many masters of this art think that when one is inquiring about a battle or some act of cruelty one should use a sword that has killed many people, because the spirits come all the more quickly and readily. When one wants to inquire about pleasure and joy, to come up with some trick, or dig for treasure, the sword should be pure and undefiled. I myself know a great prince who uses an old executioner's sword that has brought him high honor. Alas, what an evil superstition that is! How can the steel and the iron serve in these things? Believe me, that the Devil takes great pleasure in such superstition. But you, O unwise and desperate and nefarious man—whether pagan, Jew, or Christian—you will not bear in mind how grievously you anger the God who created you!

Chapter 89: About the greatest error of all in the art of pyromancy

In the art of pyromancy there are many further superstitions, and especially one which is surely the most despicable and evil, for the more firmly a person believes in such sorcery, the more of a sin it is. This practice involves having boys see future affairs and all sorts of things in a crystal. It is false, desperate, and straying Christians who make use of this practice, for the Devil's trickery and deceit is dearer to them than God's truth, in various forms. Some have a pure, fine, polished crystal or beryl, which they have consecrated and keep entirely clean, and they apply to it incense, myrrh, and such things; and when they want to exercise the art, they wait for a fine day or else they use a clean chamber with many consecrated candles. The masters then go to a bath, taking the innocent child along, and clothe themselves in a pure white garment and sit down and speak their prayers of sorcery, then they burn their offerings of sorcery, then they have the child look into the stone and whisper into his ears secret words that are supposed to be very holy. In fact, the words are devilish!

Chapter 90: How they interrogate the boy in pyromancy

After this they ask the boy if he sees an angel. If the boy says "yes," they ask him what color it displays. If the boy says "red," the masters say, "Oh dear, the angel is angry," and they pray more and make all the more offering to the evil Devil. The evil Devil is pleased by this. If the boy then says, "The angel is black," the master says, "The angel is very angry, we must pray yet more and burn more lights, so as to assuage the anger of the angel," and so they pray more and make offering with more incense and other things. Take note, O pious Christian, how great a sin it is to extend to the evil Devil the service due to almighty God. When the Devil thinks he has had enough service, he lets the angel appear in white, and then the master is happy; he asks the child then, "What does the angel have in his hand?" He keeps asking until he says, "I see a slip of paper in the angel's hand." Then he keeps asking until he sees letters; the master puts those letters together and makes words out of them, until he has what he has made inquiry about.

Chapter 91: About great superstitions in the art of pyromancy

The masters of the art are so foolish that they think they can learn from it all future and past things, and all arts, secrets, and medicine. The poor masters are badly deceived when they suppose the art involves contact with the holy angels and is no sin but a divine grace and revelation. They are badly deceived, for it is truly a superstition, and the more you fast, pray, and make sacrifice, the more you sin, since at all times you pay divine honor to the Devil, which deeply displeases God and is very much against God. Further, such honors and ceremonies are forbidden by Holy Church. When the masters bring their angels into the crystals, they keep them from all uncleanness, and they think they have gained great treasure. But that is untrue and a real deception: just watch the masters and listen to what they say, and you will find that they lie ten times before they speak the truth once. Anyone who puts his faith in such talk is a real fool.

Chapter 92: How all the masters and sorcerers use evil words and are despised

Notice also that the masters of this art are in the habit of using evil words in various ways. Thus, my highborn prince, flee from this business, because it is deceptive indeed and malicious and brings the well-being of soul and body into great peril. When the masters in this art grant release to their angel, who is really a devil, they again make use of much prayer and conjuration, and as though their first superstition and sorcery was not enough, they do it a second time. But believe me, poor master, as often as you do that, you anger God and fall into grievously mortal sin.

Chapter 93: Another form of sorcery involving crystals

There are other masters in the art who make use of their crystals quite simply and straightforwardly without fasting, praying, or keeping themselves clean with baths and with [wearing particularly clean] garments. They think that their art is the best of all, because it is carried out so simply and straightforwardly. They are as much deceived as the first group, yet their sin is smaller, because they render less honor to the Devil. You should thus know that the more you pray, make offering, and fast in such arts of sorcery, the more and the worse you anger God, who alone created you. You should give such honor only to God, and not to any Devil or to any other of his handiwork.

Chapter 94: How many priests bring about appearances of this sort in the consecrated paten

It has indeed happened that many priests have been so keen on such visions that they have taken the holy paten on which God is transformed in the mass;[81] they have had children gaze at it, believing that only the holy angels can appear in it, and no devils. They have erred greatly, because anyone who treats or makes use of holy consecrated things other than as holy Church has ordained sins greatly and is guilty of superstition, for he misuses God's order of things. Further, you should believe that these holy things do not banish the Devil, but it is only the faith and the pure prayer of Christians that drives away all evil spirits and the Devil's trickery.

---

81. Meaning transubstantiated.

Chapter 95: Another example of how the Devil is able to come close to holy things

One reads in the book of Caesarius [of Heisterbach] how a blessed monk asked the Devil where he had been.[82] He said, "I have been at Himmenrod and have waited for the soul of Brother Herman, who has died; but he has escaped from us." The monk asked, "How dare you approach to a holy man?" The Devil said, "You should not be amazed, for I was near Jesus, God's son, sitting on the left arm of the cross when he died." From this you can see the superstition of the priests who think the appearances in the paten take place through holy angels, a belief in which they are deceived.

Chapter 96: How this art is also carried out with molten lead

There is further a trick of sorcery, also included in the art of pyromancy, to which I have referred. The masters of the art take lead or tin and melt it, then pour it into water, take it out quickly, and conjure the color and the little holes in the lead or tin, and tell of future or past things on that basis. That is all a superstition, for when the metal becomes hotter, the more color it takes on, and the higher you pour it out the more pieces into which it falls. All that is natural, and no one can foretell evil or good on that basis. Those who use this for fortune-telling are no doubt not lacking in the inspiration and guidance of the Devil. Your princely grace should be on guard against this and should punish other people who engage in it.

Chapter 97: About various types of vision [not all of them] in pyromancy

There are many types of appearance called visions, not all of which belong to the art of pyromancy, but there are distinct forms of super-

---

82. Caesarius of Heisterbach, *Dialogue on Miracles*, trans. Scott and Bland, Book 12, chap. 5, 2:293–97.

stition, which I will describe later on, when I write about the other arts.[83] For now I will describe the sixth art, called chiromancy.

K. CHIROMANCY

Chapter 98: About the sixth art, called chiromancy

Chiromancy is an art in which one sees in the hand what will happen or has happened to someone—whether to children, women, or lords—or what a person can or may expect to encounter in life.[84] Mancius the Sorcerer invented this art.[85] The art involves looking at the lines in the hand, and the fingers as well as the palm, on the basis of which the master says what he is seeking to find out in the art. Looking also at the fingers, the masters predict how things will come out. However one views this art, and however one carries it out, it is a sin, forbidden, and truly a superstition.

Chapter 99: How the masters of the art themselves maintain it is true

The masters in the art of chiromancy believe their art is legitimate, and they find support in a book written by Aristotle about the forms of the human body, called *Physiognomy*,[86] and the first practitioner of the art was called Pyson. Since that book is legitimate [argue the masters], which speaks about the form and members and face, the nose, mouth, ears, eyes, and teeth, why then should not our book also

---

83. Hartlieb seems not to have carried out this plan.

84. Hartlieb wrote a separate book on this subject, *Die Kunst Chiromantia des Dr. Hartlieb, ein Blockbuch aus den siebziger Jahren des fünfzenten Jahrhunderts*, ed. Ernst Weil (Munich: Gaus, 1923). See *HDA*, vol. 2, cols. 37–56.

85. On "Mancius" see JH-1989, 148. A play on *manus*, "hand," seems plausible.

86. *HMES*, vol. 2, chap. 4, pp. 246–78 on Pseudo-Aristotle generally, and 266–67 on the *Physiognomy* in particular.

be legitimate?[87] Against that, the teachers say that the *Physiognomy* of Aristotle deals only with natural matters and speaks only about a person's inclinations according to the form of the body, and says nothing at all about a person's free will. But the art of chiromancy does not work that way; it says how many wives and children, how much fortune or misfortune one is to have, and what way a person will die, and many other superstitious things, which I will write about shortly. For that reason the art of chiromancy is forbidden, but physiognomy is not.

Chapter 100: How the masters subdivide the art of chiromancy

The masters of this art divide the hand into various parts. One part they call the *raszette*, the second they call *mensa* or table, the third they call the bed, the fourth they call the hill [or] the head. Then they give names to the many lines in the hand, calling one the life line, the second the line of the table, the third the line of the bed. Then they designate various hills on the hand, which we refer to as balls, and whenever a line cuts across a ball it is supposed to mean something. All that is trumpery, for the lines signify nothing either harmful or good.

Chapter 101: How the masters interpret the art of chiromancy

Likewise, the masters say that someone who has a broad table will become rich, someone with a long table line will be fond of eating, someone with lines in his bed will have as many wives as there are lines, and he will have as many children as there are lines in the ball of the little finger. The poor masters of this art also say that someone

---

87. *unser půch*: Eisermann and Graf suggest reading *unser kunst*, "our art," and they translate the phrase as referring to the magicians' teaching.

Clearly, in any event, the assertion is that the teaching in the magicians' books is as legitimate as that in the work of (Pseudo)-Aristotle.

with a cross on the head-ball will rise to high office. They make many such claims, but in reality there is no foundation or truth in the art. Your princely grace should thus place no faith in it. Further, Your Grace should know that the masters in the art—and especially the mistresses, since women exercise this art more than men—say that however small a "hill" on the hand or the fingers may be, each of these "hills" or "mountains" on the fingers and the hand is a point with a particular sign and meaning. They also say that one point reduces the strength and power of another. All that is a superstition, for the points and lines come when the skin is wrinkled or creased, and they signify nothing evil or good. That is what you should believe, and nothing else. If you believe something else, you are committing a mortal sin and engaged in something unchristian.

Chapter 102: How the fingers are considered in this art

You should further know that people also examine the fingers, whether the little finger extends to the upper portion of the ring finger, which is supposed to mean great fortune, and the further up it extends, the greater the fortune. In addition, if the small finger does not extend to that portion of the ring finger, then a person will be terribly unlucky. Do not concern yourself with these things, O good Christian, for they are trumpery. The length and shortness of the fingers and other members comes from natural factors and have no relevance to superstition or tricks of sorcery. Macrobius, the great teacher in occult natural arts, discusses the actual facts about greater or smaller length or shortness of all the members, and anyone who wants to know about this should read the book that Macrobius wrote about the dream of Scipio, and he will find therein more than he can ask about the proportions of natural complexion and composition.[88]

88. On Macrobius see *HMES*, vol. 1, pp. 544–45.

Chapter 103: About the Gypsies, how they trick simple people

There is a people who move around much in the world, called Gypsies. These people, women and men, children and old, exercise this art a great deal and mislead many simple folks, bringing many people to much superstition. These people are quite free in what they say. When they come upon gullible people, they induce many to believe in them. Yet in truth their art has no foundation, and they know no differences in the interpretations of hands, for they cannot name any of the lines or "hills." One must recognize that they know nothing at all. Be on guard against them, you simple, pious Christian. You who are wise, flee them also, and you will not give anyone occasion for sin.

Chapter 104: How there is no foundation in the Gypsies' art

I tell you, I have asked many of these Gypsies, even the wisest and best women and men, the most knowing, to see if they really knew anything about their art. But in fact I have never found among them any real skill in these matters, for all they care about is taking money from people or stealing the shirts off people's backs.[89] They exercise many other kinds of sorcery, all of which are trumpery. Believe me, you can ask them for anything you can think of, and they will tell you they can do it, and they tell you some lore about herbs and words [of sorcery], but they are making it all up. Therefore, esteemed prince, prevent all that in your princedom, and other princes will follow your example.

Chapter 105: How loss of temporal goods is no real harm, but harm to the soul is very great [cf. Matthew 16:26; Mark 8:36]

There is small harm in giving them food, bread, wine, meat for God's sake, and there would be small harm, too, if they were to steal food to

---

89. *oder gewandt zu laichen*: Eisermann and Graft give a similar rendering but suggest *gewinett* for *gewandt*, which would mean they are skilled at deception.

sustain themselves. But there is great harm when they introduce such superstition and sorcery, which unfortunately makes so strong an impact on many people that it is difficult to free them from it. This superstition takes root not only in common people but also among the high and mighty. For if the human mind is unstable, turning now here and now there, Satan comes along with his countless tricks to give guidance, help and instruction, counsel and deed, until he has made people firm in superstition and led them to eternal torment and damnation.

Chapter 106: About a sorceress

I myself, Doctor Hartlieb, have had a strange experience of the art of chiromancy. I came to a land with several of my friends and companions, and there I was told of a sorceress or fortune-teller who could tell of great matters and display great art, telling what a person had gone through in his life and what he would experience in the future. I paid little attention to that, for I have often heard great reports with little art behind them. But some of my good friends, including my servant and even a priest who was traveling with me, went off to the woman, who lived a considerable distance from the city where I was. When they came back, they reported great things that the woman had said to each of them in particular. Each of them swore a mighty oath that it was all true. The priest told about many things that she had said to him that no man knew. He praised her highly. I had an apothecary, a French speaker,[90] who had made trial of many things, who had been in my service for five years, in whom I placed faith and trust, and he related to me the great things she had told him about that had happened to him in Apulia. I paid no attention to all that. Many honorable people often mentioned this woman. Then an honorable and well-placed knight told me how she had given him a prediction about an important matter that proved true. After that, a territorial lord told

90. *ainen rechten walhen*, which Eisermann and Graf render as *ein geb-ürtiger Welscher.*

me that she had said to him he would gain a high ruling office, and at the time in question he did achieve great authority. I heard great things said of this woman from other people as well. Many praised her, and neither before nor after did I hear any person speak ill of her. My adoptive brother[91] was with me in that land. He asked me several times to send for the woman, because he had heard that she wished to be with me.

Chapter 107: How I myself sought counsel from the woman and was with her

After much earnest entreaty of my brother, I gave in to him and said he could summon her, but not to my house; and that is what happened. My brother showed her great courtesy and companionship, outside my house. My brother was a widely experienced man in many matters. He came to me gladly and told me how the woman had said great things that had happened to him in France. He asked me to pay her honor. I invited her as guest with other honorable women. She remained with me from morning until evening. I had much conversation with the woman, who was quite at home in the world.[92] She said the art had been in her family for many years, and after her death this gift would pass to her eldest daughter.

Chapter 108: How I realized that her art was nothing at all

There was much conversation. I asked her to share her art with me; she was willing. She had me wash my hands, and dried them with her own hands, then bent her face close to my hand and told me things that could not possibly happen to me. Then I realized clearly from what she was saying that she was telling me what I wanted to hear. In

---

91. *gesworner brůder.*
92. *die wol der welt geleich was*: Eisermann and Graf takes this as meaning Hartlieb had a long talk with the woman about God and the world (which seems to me an unlikely reading), but suggest that the text might be emended.

all respects I dealt with her properly. I am still waiting for the things to happen that she told me. But in all Christian truth I can only wonder that so many high, mighty, experienced, and honorable people, women and men, make so much of what is really nothing. Truly, truly, all this is nothing but trumpery. And if the woman told someone something that proved true, no doubt this would be from the evil spirits, whom people have with them without their knowledge, as holy Scripture says clearly and openly, as I will report when I write about the other eighty-four [arts], especially about those people who have the spirit of Python with them.[93]

Chapter 109: How the art of chiromancy is nothing but trumpery

In the art of chiromancy there are many frivolous people who believe and think the lines compel and force a person to evil or good things, as laid out in the configuration of the hand; and that is truly a superstition, for if it were so, a person would not have his own free will. All that is very much against the Christian faith. The masters and mistresses of this art of chiromancy also examine the colors of the lines when they are carrying out their art and fortune-telling. They say a person who has red lines running from above to the bottom [of the hand] will live a long life, but a person who has pale [lines] will live a short life or soon become sick. There is a particular line in every person's hand that they call the life line, and this the point where fades out indicates that the person is to die. That such statements of theirs are erroneous and superstitious can be seen from the fact that workers with hard hands have very few lines, and yet they die all the same; thus life does not depend on the hands, but rather on the strength of the heart, for many a person lives who has no hands at all.

93. Again, a plan that seems not to have been carried out.

Chapter 110: More evidence that the art is trumpery

Further, your princely grace should know that the art is nothing but trumpery. For the masters say that by the art one can foretell to any person everything he will do or have done throughout his life. But there are many who insist that for a man one should examine the right hand, and for a woman the left hand. Since many men have deformed hands from birth, or defective or crooked hands, how is one supposed to determine for these people how they will live, what they will do, and what they will have done? That cannot be done! Thus the art is not complete or perfect.

Chapter 111: That there is no way the art can be seen as legitimate

So there are many books of the masters, with nothing but trickery and a willful perversion of nature. Even if it worked in principle, still I have not been able to find either greater or lesser indications that the lines have power or mean anything in particular.[94] For the same man on one day after bathing with his hands, doing labor, or working [some operation] will have the lines changed so dramatically that they become the contrary of what they have been. For the red line becomes pale from [exposure to] cold, the pale becomes red from heat, the long becomes short from dryness, the short becomes long from moisture. In this way all the lines become changed by quite minor influences. So if the master should pass judgment according to the teaching of his art, then a single person's life would be now short, now long, now sick, now healthy, all within a brief span of time. What an error that is, and so Your Grace will realize that that the art is nothing but made-up trumpery and superstition, with which the Devil draws and leads frivolous people into his net and company.

94. JH-1914 refers to this, understandably, as a problematic sentence.

Chapter 112: Another art and evil deception exercised in the art of chiromancy

The great masters and mistresses carry out something else that I have encountered even more often. This exercise involves looking at the fingernails of each person.[95] They say that the fingers blossom and acquire spots; these spots signify the person's fortune or misfortune, death or life, wealth or poverty, and such things about which people inquire. The masters and mistresses make many distinctions; first they distinguish the colors of these spots on the nails, then whether they are round or broad, long or narrow, also whether they extend to the side or toward the body. They make a particular judgment according to each such condition, as their art and mastery teaches. But if we were to speak the actual truth, it is mere trumpery and superstition, since such spots come from the moisture of the body, which comes out in a natural manner, and signifies nothing beyond what is natural, neither fortune nor misfortune, neither death nor life.

Chapter 113: How the masters of medicine base their art on true nature and pass judgment on that basis

In the art of medicine there is indeed this cause of death, as Avicenna writes, that all people must die by consumption of natural moisture or by excessive moisture that reduces the natural heat.[96] Anyone who wants to know about that should read the aforementioned chapter. All that has nothing to do with the hand and its lines. So, too, the great master Hippocrates, in whose words nothing false or untrue has ever been found, wrote a book on death and health called *The Prognostics of Hippocrates*, in which one finds how a person's illness will end well or badly, in death or life.[97] In all that, he and all the following masters

95. *HDA*, vol. 2, col. 1500.

96. *Flores Avicenne collecti super quinque canonibus*, ed. Michael de Capella (Lyon: Gilbert de Villiers, 1514), fol. 20[r–v].

97. Hippocrates, *Pronostic*, ed. and trans. Jacques Jouanna, Anargyros Anastassiou, and Caroline Magdelaine (Paris: Les Belles Lettres, 2013); Hippocrates, *The Prognostics and Crises*, trans. Henry William Ducachet (New York: Eastburn, 1819).

of medicine acknowledge the first cause, which has ordered all things, that being the Lord God, who holds all things in his hand and ordains and disposes them according to the will of his divine majesty.

Chapter 114: That one can recognize that such arts are deception

Thus one can clearly realize that all such arts, especially those presuming to coerce the human free will, are nothing but trumpery. And this is superstition by which a person angers God, the spouse of his soul, who wishes to have no falsehood or suspicion in his spouse, but a true, firm, and full Christian faith. May Jesus Christ, the son of Mary and God, who saved and redeemed us by his holy passion, deign to grant and confirm this for you, for me, and for all Christians. Amen. Let that be enough about the art of chiromancy. Now I will tell and write about the seventh forbidden art, called in Latin *spatulamancia*.

L. SPATULAMANCY

Chapter 115: About the seventh art, called spatulamancy

Spatulamancy is one of the seven forbidden arts.[98] The art involves use of a strange and disconcerting form of trickery, and although I have given much attention to all the arts, I have never found any superstition with less foundation than this art. It is indeed a ridiculous art, and it could never have been dreamed up except to enable the evil Devil to tempt simple people and lead them astray in all things.[99] The masters of this art take the shoulder blade of a dead ox or horse, cow or ass—I have asked if they could tell fortunes from the shoulder blade of a human, which should be the best, but [they said] the shoulder blades of all large animals are quite good—and they wash these shoulder

98. Kieckhefer, *Forbidden Rites*, 113; *HDA*, vol. 8, cols. 125–40.

99. Eisermann and Graf find the text difficult and possibly corrupt, but the basic meaning seems clear.

blades well with wine, then with holy water, and wrap them up in a pure cloth.

Chapter 116: How the art proceeds

And when they want to carry out their art and trick of sorcery, they bind up the shoulder blades and take them to a place outdoors, and examine the shoulder blades, and they believe the shoulder blades change after each question. They use neither a [ceremonial] light nor an offering, but it is a great superstition that they wash the shoulder blades with holy water and that they believe the shoulder blades change and transform themselves in accordance with their questions. The masters' faith is so great that they make no inquiry into the foundation of this art. They speak freely everything that occurs to them by way of answers and solutions to their questions.

Chapter 117: How greatly the masters in this art err

They are so very much beclouded in their senses and so afflicted in their reason that they believe they can and should make inquiry into all questions, whether about death, life, honor or goods, riches or poverty, affliction or health, leaving nothing out, neither the rising or falling prices of crops, coldness, snow, water or dryness of the earth— what more could one want? And in all truth there is no other foundation than that the evil Devil involves himself and suggests such answers and understanding to these foolish masters. And I will write and reveal to your princely grace how and in what way the Devil brings it about that the master remains unaware that this is all the Devil's teaching and deception.

Chapter 118: How the Devil cannot coerce the human senses

It was mentioned above that the Devil cannot coerce the senses or mind of any human, yet he so allures people that he can introduce into their minds likenesses and appearances, so that simple people feel themselves compelled and think it cannot be any other way. He can also arouse in the imagination things that previously lay deeply submerged, so that these frivolous people perceive images and likenesses from them. Then the masters of spatulamancy say that such examples and likenesses show what is true and will actually happen, then the Devil affords help and counsel with all his tricks, so that he misleads and misguides the master and the people who believe in his art. And since the Devil cannot do anything but what God allows him, you should know this: when God sees that you, O frivolous one, are not willing to believe in him, and that you despise and disdain his teaching, which the blessed priests impart, and further do not believe the holy Scriptures and are not willing to follow them, then he will allow it to happen that you and your master are misguided and misled.

Chapter 119: How foolish those people who believe in such an art

O you poor, senseless, silly man, what do you have in mind when you deny your God, who made you, and redeemed you with the shedding of his holy blood and his great bitter passion and death, and bind and ally yourself with your superstition and sorcery to the archenemy of yourself and all the children of humankind, the evil Devil, who as a reward will give you eternal suffering and torment? Oh, what an uneven exchange you have made, giving up the eternal joy of God and his wondrous everlasting life for eternal suffering and torment! Repent, poor man, and take as help the mother of all mercy, and ask for grace, have contrition, make confession, do penance, so God may yet have mercy on you!

Chapter 120: How this art involves, and what [the masters] mostly attend to

The masters of this art also take pains to examine what color the shoulder blade has at the end, in the middle, and in all places. Then the Devil suggests to them what they should think and say. The Devil's tricks are without number, and so, too, are the practices of this art, so no one could recount them all. Yet I will write about certain practices, as far as I know them, which belong to this damned art, telling the claims the masters of spatulamancy make for themselves and their art, all of which are great superstition.

Chapter 121: About the superstition involving use of a goose bone

First I will write about the [use of a] goose bone.[100] When people have eaten a goose on Saint Martin's Day or Eve, the oldest and wisest keep the breastbone and let it dry out until early in the morning, then they look at it from all angles, in front and behind and in the middle. From it they judge how the winter will be, whether cold or warm, dry or moist, and they believe so firmly that they will bet their property on it. They use it for a special form of fortune-telling, which cannot go wrong, by which they predict whether the snowfall will be heavy or light. All that can come from the goose bone! In times gone by, the old peasants practiced this sort of thing on their remote farms, but now the superstition has spread among kings, princes, and the entire nobility, who believe in such things. I scarcely dare mention the clergy, since they want to punish but remain unpunished—and yet I know quite a few great prelates, archbishops, abbots, provosts, and many other quite honorable priests, who are generally irreproachable in their life and order, but who believe in the goose bone. And shortly I will prove that the belief in the bone and its significance for the winter is trumpery, although there are certain signs to be seen in birds and animals from which one can draw some inferences about changes in the weather. That is a natural matter, and Albert the Great wrote much about that in his book called *De signis serenitatis pluvie*, about which I will speak shortly.[101]

---

100. *HDA*, vol. 3, cols. 290–95, especially 293.

101. Hartlieb is referring to a work in the tradition of Theophrastus of Ere-

sus, *On Winds and on Weather Signs*, trans. James G. Wood, ed. G. J. Symons (London: Stanford, 1894).

Chapter 122: Why a goose bone has no meaning beyond the natural

A goose bone is supposed to be especially good and certain, something that does not go wrong. But say, good man, how do you know if that is true or not? The goose bone has six dimensions: below itself, above itself, behind itself, before itself, to the left, and to the right; but all bodily things have the same. The goose bone also has various colors, but other bodies have the same. You may say it depends on its watery and earthly nature, but other birds and animals have that, too, such as ducks, herons, blackbirds, and animals such as beavers, crabs, seals, and otters. Why does no one write about these? Believe me, esteemed prince, this superstition is a delusion of the Devil, and furthermore it is uncertain, always teetering between yes and no. No one, therefore, will ever find any truth in these matters.

Chapter 123: How one can gain knowledge of these matters from nature

Yet according to the true, natural course and conjunction of the stars, which bring into play the influence of cold and moist, dry and warm stars, the wise stargazers can indeed discern and know the circumstances of the four seasons, winter, spring, summer, and autumn. But that does not come from the goose [bone]; in truth, the goose has misled many people! Guard yourself, O Christian prince, that you, too, are not misguided and misled, for their allurements are sweet.[102]

Chapter 124: A good lesson in how one must be on guard against the Devil's deception

O esteemed prince, I will tell you the whole truth: all this business is nothing other than the Devil's deception. Just as the Devil misleads

---

102. *wann ir peissen sind süß*: Eisermann and Graf follow the variant *speyß*, "food," which is a plausible reading, but I have made the text slightly less determinate, while preserving basically the same point.

frivolous people by means of many things, he does so also by means of the goose. My brother-in-law, when the Devil suggests to someone that the goose and many [other] birds change according to the weather, as mentioned above, that has no basis, for when geese are all eaten one night, they have been quite differently raised and fed, so how could they all have the same meaning? Truly, truly, do not concern yourself with such things, for the Devil is master in these matters and carries out his trickery.

Chapter 125: What nature changes and transforms

Your Grace knows full well that food, air, constraints, needs, and so forth will affect the conditions of nature, as Galen writes in his Book 2.[103] Your Grace also knows well that the goose is fed with many kinds of things, as the peasant women with whom you have often met in confidence may perhaps have told you. One goose is fed with oats, another with turnips, another with barley, another with bran, and one is stuffed while another is put in a pot,[104] one is fed high up under a roof, another in a crib in the cellar. Your high understanding will thus well grasp that this goose bone does not have power from nature, since each manner of feeding will give the goose and its bone a different nature. Without doubt it is a trickery of the Devil, who has often led these poor people astray with fasting and discipline, but now wants to mislead, misguide, and damn them with overindulgence. Oh dear, what wondersome wiles and cunning he can deploy!

Chapter 126: A sad lamentation over such sorcery

O my dear, sweet Lord Jesus, why do you allow all this, or why do you suffer that the evil Devil befools and beguiles your hard-won people? Bestow grace on your creatures and keep them from being misled, for the sake of your holy name Jesus. Amen.

---

103. On Galen see *HMES*, vol. 2, pp. 117–81.

104. *aine plent man, die ander setzt man in ainen hafen*: here I follow Eisermann and Graf.

Chapter 127: Another evil superstition in the art of spatulamancy

Spatulamancy involves another of the Devil's evil tricks, that often a person sees some thing and becomes terrified, saying, "Today I will have no luck!" That is surely a superstition and a trick of the Devil. In this art there is also the superstition that people often say, "Oh, this or that person has cursed my child or my horse, so it will never again put on weight or grow, but will have to shrivel up and waste away!" O esteemed prince, you should put no faith in that, for it is a heresy and very much against God.

Chapter 128: What imps, cormorants, and changelings are[105]

The natural physicians know well about these things, and say there is a sickness called *bolismus* or *appetitus caninus*.[106] This illness cannot be cured with any eating or drinking alone, because all food goes undigested through the body, and so the flesh wastes away while the bones retain their size. This causes children to become deformed, and they are called changelings.

Chapter 129: More about changelings

I will describe for your princely grace something that I have not found written in any reliable writing, but I have heard it said by women more than man that such changelings, when they arrive at three years or thereabouts, have disappeared from the eyes of honorable women and

105. *was der götz und vil fräß und wächselkind sey*; see JH-1989, 144.

106. Hans Kunroth and Sherman M. Kuhn, eds., *Middle English Dictionary* (Ann Arbor: University of Michigan Press, 1952–), vol. B, p. 1029, from John of Trevisa's translation of Bartholomew de Glanville, *De proprietatibus rerum*: "Bolismus is in moderat & vnmesurable, as it were an houndis appetite . . . Aȝþenst þis euel bolismus, hote þing schal be take þat comfortiþ þe stomake," and "Houndes haueþ continual bolysme . . . and beþ somtyme so punysched wiþ hunger, þat þay waxeþ rabbissh and woode." See also *HDA*, vol. 9, cols. 862–63.

men and been lost forever. However that may be, in the end it is the opinion of holy Scripture that the One who knows all hearts knows well how certain people find such love and comfort in their children that they forget God and the grace he has formerly given them. Now God does not wish that they be lost. He withdraws their joy from them so they will think again on him, and for the sake of the sin that the father and mother have committed against him God will punish them, laying such shame on them. That is the opinion of holy Scripture.

Chapter 130: Another story about the goose bone

I want to tell you something else about the goose bone that a great victorious [army] captain told me recently, a man in whom great princes and common folk all put great trust, one for his deeds, another for his wisdom, the third for his loyalty, which he maintained at all times and in all perils toward his hereditary prince. This good man said to me within this year, on Saint Nicholas Day, 1455, "Dear master, how will the winter be this year, according to what you stargazers say?" I spoke out boldly, as I still tend to do, and said, "My lord, Saturn is entering this month into a fiery sign, and the other stars are following after, so in three years there will not be a harsh winter." This tried and tested man, this Christian captain, took out of his clothing that heretical superstition, the goose bone, and said to me that after Candlemas there would be deep cold, without fail. Whatever I said, he came back at me, and told me the Teutonic Knights in Prussia had planned all their wars with the aid of the goose bone, and as the goose bone had indicated, so they carried out their two campaigns, one in summer, the other in winter. He said more to this effect, that so long as the Teutonic Knights followed the [goose] bone, they had great standing and honor; but since they had stopped, God knows how it goes with them.

Chapter 131: An answer to the previous chapter

I said, "If the Teutonic Knights have no other art, aid, and guidance than the goose bone, then they don't have much confidence." With that I departed from my wealthy host and lamented again and again that he had such faith in the goose bone. But by God's grace the winter was quite mild, and the goose that had misled him has again this year failed, up to Reminiscere Sunday.[107] I trust it will continue to fail. You may say, "If the entire operation and everything of the sort is so untenable, how does it come about that the common people believe in it so much?" The holy teachers answer that there are certain signs in nature that signify either rain or sunshine, but these signs may be wrong, although they may also prove true.

M. GENERAL PROHIBITION

Chapter 132: That such arts are forbidden by Holy Church

When the evil Devil, the malign enemy of all humankind, realized the frivolity of humans, and saw that more and more of them were following such signs, taking superstition for true love of God and for his commandment, he involved himself in these matters and gave guidance and help in them, so that these frivolous people fell yet more deeply into superstition and became totally immersed in it. Holy Church took note of that, and saw the great loss of souls, and strictly forbade all such arts, sorcery and superstition, under penalty of fire, in her *Decretals.* In secular laws as well these arts are strictly forbidden, for the books say that such sorcery and idolatry should be torn out with glowing tongs and hooks, without clemency or mercy, as is written in the law books.

I will list and specify other torments and punishments appropriate to such sorcerers and seducers at the end of this book, and I will give proof on the basis of Scriptures, where it is all written.

Clara Hätzlerin[108]

---

107. The second Sunday of Lent.
108. Scribe who wrote the manuscript containing Hartlieb's work. She was born ca. 1430, lived in Augsburg, and died after 1476. See JH-1989, 144.

On Witches and Pythonesses, in German "Unholden" or "Hexen"

ULRICH MOLITORIS

A treatise addressed to the most illustrious prince, lord Sigismund, archduke of Austria, Styria, Carinthia, et cetera, on witches (*laniae*)[1] and pythonesses, by Ulrich Molitoris of Constance, doctor of canon law from Pavia, and advocate of cases before the court of Constance, written in honor of that prince and subject to the correction of his highness.

LETTER

Most excellent prince and lord, most venerable lord archduke, the humble Ulrich Molitoris, doctor of Constance, offers himself in service to your highness. For some years a plague of witches and enchantresses is said to have invaded the lands of Your Excellency. Some women suspected of this heresy were captured under your authority, and upon being interrogated under torture they gave various responses. Your counselors held various opinions among themselves on this matter, one leaning in one direction, another in a different direction, and at last your clemency recalled my name. Thus, for your inborn eagerness to know the truth, I have received a commission through your worthiness's counselors to set down assiduously in writing for Your Excellency what I believe in this matter. I do so, although this may be burdensome and dangerous. It is burdensome in particular for me as I am engaged in other business and

---

1. For the term *lania*, see *"Etymologies" of Isidore of Seville*, trans. Barney et al., bk. 8, chap. 11, sec. 99, p. 190.

FIGURE 1 Presentation of the dialogue to Archduke Sigismund from Ulrich Molitoris, *De laniis et phitonicis mulieribus* (Reutlingen: Johann Otmar, ca. 1489), sig. a iᵛ.

seeking to obtain a means of living. And it is dangerous on account of those envious detractors who are always slinging criticism at what they cannot themselves achieve, and the things that they themselves in their laziness could not have undertaken they never fail to rip apart with venomous teeth like some bristly goat.[2] This material brings even learned teachers into doubt, yet I have decided it is fitting that, for Your Excellency's sake, not only the members of my feeble body should be devoted to your service, but you should have also the powers of my mind, such as they are. Thus, while the parts of the outer man devote themselves to your service, my weak and unculti-vated intellect as well may rouse itself for the glory of your highness. I submit the present work, therefore, subject to correction from you and your wise counselors, especially that of the most illustrious Conrad Sturtzel, doctor of both laws and chief secretary of Your Excellency, for whose correction I have in particular submitted this treatise. I have done so because in days gone by he was my preceptor and teacher of eloquence, from whom as a young man I imbibed the elements and the principles of law, and I would gladly imbibe from him today as well. And since among orators of former times the dialogue was often taken to be a pleasant form, thus in the present treatise I have decided to proceed by way of a dialogue, or rather a trialogue. On the matter at hand I have heard a great deal that is worth discussion from the wise and eminent Conrad Schatz, who has served many years as judge and magistrate in this great city of mine, Constance. He is a man highly distinguished and renowned for his eloquence, and as judge he has heard the confession of these women. I have therefore decided to construct the present dialogue or tria-logue using the names of Your Excellency, this Conrad, and myself, proceeding thus to the matter at hand, with your kind indulgence.[3] First, however, I have set forth certain questions as keys to the mate-rial under discussion.

2. On this passage see UM-1997, 113nn2–5.

3. On these individuals see UM-1997, 113n4; on Konrad Stürzel see Mauz, *Ulrich Molitoris*, 36, 38, 42, 53, 60, 75–76.

THE CHAPTERS OF THE PRESENT TREATISE

1. Whether by the action of witches and enchantresses, with the cooperation of demons, hail and frost and rain can be aroused to harm the earth.
2. Whether witches and enchantresses are able with the help of the Devil to harm men and little children, inflicting illnesses on them and undermining their health.
3. Whether they can undermine a man's power of coition, even if he is in the state of marriage, and make him impotent.
4. Whether they can change the appearances and faces of men into other forms.
5. Whether enchantresses and witches can ride on an anointed stick or on a wolf or some other animal, and be taken from place to place, going to the place of their assembly, where they drink, and eat, and have [carnal] knowledge and take carnal delight with one another.
6. Whether the Devil can have sex with bewitching women of this sort, lying with them in the form of a man.
7. Whether children can be begotten of such coition.
8. Whether enchantresses and pythonesses are able with the help of demons to know secret things, to reveal the counsels of princes, and to predict future events.
9. Whether by just judgment such bewitching and miscreant women can be burned or subjected to other punishments.[4]

PART I

1. The most gracious Archduke Sigismund of Austria begins the dialogue

Sigismund. Doctor Ulrich, you are dear and faithful to us, and you enjoy singular favor for the services you have rendered us, so we have

---

4. The ninth chapter is not actually given as such; the material assigned to it is discussed at the end of the dia- logue, in the section here labeled as an epilogue.

chosen you in preference to others to hold a disputation about the present subject.

Ulrich. Illustrious prince, it is flattering that in your kindness to me you should judge me worthy to take part in this disputation. But Conrad Schatz, judge in my city, is at hand—a man of great intelligence, acute in conversation, and a good friend of mine. So may it please you to learn first of all about the efforts he has made in this matter.

Sigismund. That seems good to me, for I know that he is mature in counsel and fine in conversation. And so, since we are to speak about the bewitchments of witches and enchantresses, I want first to ask whether thunderstorms, rain, and hail can be aroused by the action of witches.

Conrad. In so difficult a matter as this, which causes even the most learned men to shy away from expressing themselves, I must acknowledge my own ignorance, for as Socrates was accustomed to say, he knew only that he did not know,[5] but still, lest I seem unwilling to yield to the entreaties of my gracious prince, I shall say a few things as a way of moving the discussion to greater things.

Sigismund. Speak, then.

Conrad. It is a commonplace saying among philosophers, that the opinion everyone shares should not be altogether dismissed.[6] And it is common opinion that these witches (*strige*)[7] cause thunder and hail and bring great damage to crops and humans. From their confessions, too, made under torture, we know that they have done such things and revealed how they do them.

Sigismund. Yet I am not persuaded by public rumor alone, for people are quick to take up what they hear said. Nor am I content

5. Plato, *Apology*, 21d, in *The Dialogues of Plato*, trans. B. Jowett, vol. 1, 4th ed. (Oxford, UK: Clarendon, 1953), 345.

6. Aristotle, *Nicomachean Ethics*, I 8, 1098b, trans. E. W. Webster

(Oxford, UK: Clarendon, 1923); *The Complete Works of Aristotle*, trans. Barnes, 3732–33.

7. *SM*, bk. 3, pt. 1, dist. 6, col. 890.

with confession made under torture, since by fear of torments a person is sometimes induced to confess what is contrary to the nature of things. In any event, the things we do not see with our eyes, we desire to establish by authority or by rational demonstration, for it is by proper disputation, authority, and reason that we reach a conclusion.

Ulrich. Indeed, experience is not to be contemned in the deciding of issues, for experience is called the mistress of things, as is said in the canon *Ubi periculum*,[8] and then there is the proverbial saying, "Take it from Rupert—he's got experience."[9]

Sigismund. There is a factor that moves me to argue that witches (*laniae*) and sorceresses know nothing of all this. For if these accursed women knew about such things and were able to bring them about, it would not be necessary for princes to lead their retinues and soldiers in time of war, having them invade the lands of the enemy and devastate fields and set fire to homes and villages. It would be enough to summon such a pythoness and give her safe conduct, urging this accursed woman to arouse hail, thunderbolts, and tempests in the enemy's lands, thus threatening those lands with peril. But we see that they cannot manage such things, even if they wished, and even if they should be incited by princes to do them—perish the thought!—so I think we can conclude that they are unable to do these things. Furthermore, we have it on faith that God alone governs the stars and the elements, and commands the stars to submit to law. And according to Boethius in his book *On Consolation* he governs the world by eternal reason, and while remaining stable sets all things in motion.[10] How then could these witches with the aid of demons impede with their own motion in such matters that highest mover who governs all things by certain reason, and bring them into a different motion?

8. Molitoris refers to a canon in the *Decretals*, Sext., bk. 1, tit. 6, chap. 3, given in *CIC*, vol. 2, cols. 946–49, which actually is of little relevance.

9. Georg Büchmann, *Geflügelte Worte: Der Zitatenschatz des deutschen Volkes*, 23rd ed., rev. Eduard Ippel (Berlin: Haude & Spener, 1907), 401, cites versions of *Experto credite* from Virgil, Cicero, and Ovid, and gives a passage from Luther's correspondence in which *Experto crede Ruperto* is taken as a proverb. Not all editions of Büchmann are as thorough as this one.

10. Boethius, *Consolation of Philosophy*, bk. 3, poem 9, Green trans., 60.

Conrad. The great prince's reasoning is certainly worth considering— but no less to be taken into account is a passage from Exodus [8:1–19]. For although Moses before the face of King Pharaoh of Egypt had performed many signs and wonders, nonetheless the sorcerers did similar things when by their incantations they turned water into blood and brought forth frogs on the land. It is clear, therefore, from the scriptural witness of the Old Testament, that sorcerers by the aid of demons disturbed the waters, for they turned them into blood and devastated fields and farms with frogs. So, too, in Job [1:18–19], we read that at the Devil's instigation a strong wind rushed from the desert region and shook the four corners of Job's house, which fell, crushing and killing his children. This shows how the Devil had power to stir up the wind and crush the children. And it is said in the same book that the Devil provoked fiery thunderbolts. For the text says, "God's fire fell from heaven, and it consumed the sheep and the children it touched." Likewise, John in the Apocalypse [7:1–4] says, "After this I saw angels standing on the four corners of the earth holding the four winds of the earth lest they blow upon the earth, or the sea, or any tree, and I saw another angel rising up from the East, having the seal of the living God, and he cried out with a loud voice to the four angels to whom it was given to harm the earth and the sea, saying, `Do not harm the earth or the sea or the trees until we sign the servants of God on their foreheads.'"

Sigismund. Doctor [Ulrich], who are those four angels to whom, according to John, it was given to harm the earth?

Ulrich. They are devils.

Sigismund. Is a devil called an angel?

Ulrich. Yes, here and elsewhere a devil is often called an angel, because he, too, [like the other angels] is sent by God, as the *Glossa ordinaria* says in this regard.

Sigismund. Perhaps John saw all these things [only] in the spirit, and gave us images derived from what he saw there.

Conrad. Most worthy prince, images are not needed when the thing itself exists before our eyes, as you have heard concerning the magicians in the presence of Pharaoh, and in the acts of Job. If we read then that these things took place, then who can doubt that they can take place now as well?

Ulrich. Let us come back and address this issue more clearly at the end.[11]

2. On the harms and illnesses inflicted on people, even infants

Sigismund. Since we are speaking about the corruption and disturbance of the elements, it seems fitting to ask if they can also inflict illnesses on humans, especially infants, and harm them with the aid of demons.

Conrad. I have heard from many women how various illnesses have fallen upon children lying in their cradles—one child has a crooked nose, another has an eye torn out. And sometimes when accursed women are arrested they have confessed and acknowledged under torture that with the aid of demons they have inflicted such things on children out of ill will toward their parents.

Sigismund. You have heard that I am not persuaded by these confessions extorted by fear [of torture]. What else can you provide by way of rational proof or authority?

Conrad. Already above by way of authority in Job 1[:19] we have seen that the Devil attacked Job's sons by arousing a wind, and they died. And you should take note of what Augustine says, in his book *On the City of God*:[12] "It is written, 'The sons of Adam bear a heavy yoke from the day of their exit from their mother's womb up to the day they are buried [in the earth], the mother of all' [Ecclesiasticus 40:1]. It is even necessary that children, already released by the through the cleansing of [baptismal] regeneration from the bond of original sin by which alone they were held, should still suffer many things, and many should suffer the attacks of malign spirits." Augustine clearly believes children suffer the attacks of demons. Likewise Saint Jerome in his letter to

---

11. In what is here labeled Part II.

12. Augustine, *City of God*, bk. 21, chap. 14, Dyson trans., 1072–73.

FIGURE 2 Witch shooting a man with an arrow to make him lame, from *De laniis et phitonicis mulieribus*, sig. a iiij[v].

Paula on the dormition of Blesilla says, "What is the reason why infants two or three years old, and even those nursing at their mothers' breasts, are often afflicted by a demon?"[13] And so it can be seen from holy Scripture and the authority of the holy Fathers that a devil has the power to afflict and to harm infants and children.

Sigismund. We have spoken now about infants, but what about adults and old people?

Conrad. We have seen many old people lame and withered who assert that their condition came from the bewitchment of those accursed women.

Sigismund. But what does Scripture teach?

Conrad. In the legend of Saints Simon and Jude[14] we read how the sorcerers Zarocht and Arphaxat were set before the king of Babylon and they made that king's orators and rhetoricians mute and lame and blind, and then restored to them vision and the power of walking, which is clear evidence that sorcerers can harm men, even in advanced age, making them lame and blind and then healing them.

Sigismund. But these orators to whom such bewitchments were done were pagans. They did not believe in Christ and were not fortified by the sign of the cross.

Ulrich. You speak wisely, O illustrious prince, for in the same legend we hear how after these orators and rhetors believed in Christ and were fortified with the sign [of the cross] by the apostles those magicians were no longer able to harm them, even though the magicians tried to do so again in their exasperation.

Conrad. Well then,[15] how was the Devil able to harm Job, afflicting him with a grievous ulcer and injuring him so badly that he lay on a

---

13. Jerome, Letter 39, para. 2, in Saint Jerome, *Letters and Select Works*, trans. W. H. Fremantle, new ed. (A Select Library of Nicene and Post-Nicene Fathers of the Christian Church, ser. 2, vol. 6) (Grand Rapids, MI: Eerdmans, 1954), 50.

14. Jacobus de Voragine, *Golden Legend*, 2:262–64. Note that a question about Scripture is answered on the basis of hagiography.

15. The Latin here is *Aie aie*; the German is *Wolan wolan*.

dung heap, scarcely able to breathe, as we read in the book of Job [Job 2:7–8], although Job was a holy man, walking in the will of God, as Scripture attests. So, too, in the legend of Saint Anthony we read how demons afflicted him quite grievously,[16] yet he was a holy man and pleasing to God. So it is clear that demons had power to bring harm even to holy men. And if they were able to disturb holy men, why then would they not be able to harm others whose holiness is not evident to us?

Sigismund. From all this I find myself more and more in doubt, and so I would like to hear what opinion to hold about these things.

Ulrich. Let us break off for now,[17] and toward the end let us lay out more fully what we should make of this and other matters.

3. Whether they can cause impotence

Sigismund. Our earlier discussion brings us to another question, whether they are able to afflict a married man and render him sexually impotent.

Conrad. We have seen many fine fellows who have little or no capacity for sex, and indeed they are unable to have sex with their own wives, and they maintain that this happened to them by bewitchment.

Sigismund. O, many people say all sorts of things!

Ulrich. Yet the canon laws agree on this point, saying it can be brought about by bewitchments that a man who is not frigid by nature is made incapable of sex, and thus in the *Decretum* we have a section specifically "On those who are frigid and bewitched." Hincmar, also the pope, in the canon *Si per sortiarias*, says, "If by sorcery and the arts of bewitchment, with the permission of God's mysterious yet never unjust judgment, and by the Devil's agency, sex cannot take place, those to whom this happens should be urged to make sincere confession of all their sins to

---

16. Compare the translation in Jacobus de Voragine, *Golden Legend*, 2:93–94.

17. *Sine modo*, a phrased used in Matthew 3:15 in the Vulgate.

God and to a priest with contrite heart and a spirit of humility, et cetera."[18] Note that the text says "by the Devil's provision sex cannot take place." And although this canon should suffice to resolve this doubt in favor of belief, since the canonical constitutions should be accepted by all, as is said in the first chapter *On Constitutions*,[19] nonetheless the doctors [of theology] add their support. Thus Saint Thomas in his commentary on the *Sentences* says that by bewitchment a person can become impotent with one woman and not another. So, too, Lord Hostiensis in his *Summa*, "On those who are frigid and bewitched," says that sometimes men are bewitched in such a way that by sorcery they are rendered impotent with all women except one. Sometimes, too, they are bewitched in such a way that they cannot have sex with their wives, but they can with all other women.[20]

Sigismund. I find these things disturbing. They are so surprising, for sex is given to us by nature, and it must surely be a source of astonishment how the Devil can impede the course of nature without our awareness.

Ulrich. And yet I myself, Ulrich, have spent eighteen years in the court at Constance as lawyer and advocate in legal cases, as I am today, and in my practice I have encountered many cases of frigidity and bewitchment where in the judge's presence women have charged their husbands with sexual impotence.

Sigismund. What then was decided in these cases?

18. *Decretum*, pt. 2, case 33, qu. 1, chap. 4, given in *CIC*, vol. 1, col. 1150. Molitoris's wording is *unde Hismarus etiam papa*, for which the German translation gives *da hismarus der pabst*. The canon in question comes from Hincmar of Reims, and Gratian points out differences between this passage and a letter of Pope Gregory the Great, but Molitoris evidently construes Gregory as in fundamental agreement with Hincmar, and the German text conflates the two authors, which raises doubt about whether Molitoris himself can have done the translation.

19. *Decretals*, bk. 1, tit. 2, chap. 1, in *CIC*, vol. 2, col. 7. In context it is clear that the canon is referring to judicial actions, not doctrinal matters.

20. Catherine Rider, *Magic and Impotence in the Middle Ages* (Oxford, UK: Oxford University Press, 2006), discusses Hincmar (31–42), *Si per sortiarias* (56–58, 118–22), Thomas Aquinas (147, 154–56), and Hostiensis (115, 126), and gives the sources.

Ulrich. The judges ordered the men who were thus afflicted to show themselves to physicians sworn to the court's service,[21] so these physicians could examine them.

Sigismund. And what came of this?

Ulrich. I knew many who, inspected by these physicians who were sworn to the court's service, of whom these physicians affirmed that they were not frigid by nature but had been bewitched by sorcery.

Sigismund. And in the end what was the court's determination based on the doctors' examination?

Ulrich. The judges ordered that the parties should cohabit with each other for three years, attempting to have carnal relations, and they should be zealous in fasting and almsgiving, so that God, who is the founder of matrimony, might deign to remove this bewitchment from them. But I intend to state my own opinion about this matter more fully at the end, along with other unresolved issues, so meanwhile why do you not turn to other points of doubt, if you please.

Sigismund. There was a fourth question.

4. Whether they can change the appearances of men into other forms, and so forth

Ulrich. What do you yourself think, most worthy prince?

Sigismund. I think they cannot.

Ulrich. What moves you to say this?

Sigismund. It is said in the *Decretum*, in the canon *Episcopi*, "Whoever then believes it possible that any creature can be changed or transformed, whether for better or for worse, into any other species or

---

21. Molitoris refers twice to *medicos curie iuratos*, which could be rendered "physicians sworn to the court's service" (perhaps over a lasting term of responsibility) or "physicians sworn in by the court" (for service in a single trial).

FIGURE 3 Witches in animal form, flying, from *De laniis et phitonicis mulieribus*, sig. a vij^r.

likeness, except by the creator himself who made all things and by whom all things were made, is an infidel and worse than a pagan."[22]

Conrad. I do not propose to contradict the canon, but I want to recount what I recall having read in the works of the history writers.[23] What can one say then to Virgil, who in the *Buccolics* tells that when Ulysses went in exile from Troy with his companions he had turned to Queen Circe, and Circe on receiving them as guests had witch's potions [*pocula malefica*] administered to them, and when these guests had drunk these poisoned potions they were changed into the forms of various animals, one into a wolf, another a boar, yet another a lion.[24]

Sigismund. You are telling a fable! Those poets made things up that cannot be believed.

Conrad. But we certainly cannot dismiss the poets out of hand, for Celius Lactantius says they wrote histories, veiling them beneath hidden figures.[25] The Catholic teacher Boethius himself says as much in book 4 of *On Consolation*:[26]

> The sails of the Neritian leader [Ulysses]
> and his wandering ships
> Eurus [the east wind] drove to the island
> where the beautiful goddess [Circe] dwelt,
> begotten of the Sun.
> She mixed for her new guests
> potions infused with a charm,
> by which her hand, clever with herbs,

22. *Decretum*, pt. 2, case 26, qu. 5, chap. 12, in *CIC*, vol. 1, cols. 1030–31; P. G. Maxwell-Stuart, *Witch Beliefs and Witch Trials in the Middle Ages: Documents and Readings* (London: Continuum, 2011), 47–48.

23. Molitoris's term here is *historiographos*, which he clearly construes more broadly than our modern "historians"; in effect it means "storytellers," leaving unspecified whether the stories are fact or fiction.

24. Virgil, *Eclogues*, Eclogue 8, line 70, trans. Len Krisak (Philadelphia:

University of Pennsylvania Press, 2010), 62–63, actually a passing reference.

25. Lactantius's point is picked up by Isidore and Vincent; on the tradition see G[iovanni] Giovannini, "History and Poetry," in *Princeton Encyclopedia of Poetry and Poetics*, enlarged ed., ed. Alex Preminger, Frank J. Warnke, and O. B. Hardison, Jr. (Princeton, NJ: Princeton University Press, 1974), 348–52 (esp. 349).

26. Boethius, *Consolation of Philosophy*, bk. 4, poem 3.

turned them into various forms.
One had the face of a boar;
another, as an African lion,
grew fangs and claws.
When one, just changed into a wolf,
set out to weep, he howled.
Like a tiger of India, one
prowled meekly about the houses.
And while the winged god of Arcadia [Mercury]
took pity on the leader
beset with so many evils,
and spared him the hostess's infection,
his oarsmen had already
quaffed the evil potions.
Now as pigs they turned
to acorns as their fodder.
And nothing remained unaffected:
with voices and bodies lost,
only their minds remained unchanged
and bemoaned the monstrosities they suffered.
O how feeble the hand
and how powerless the plants
which can pervert the [outer] members
but cannot pervert the [inner] heart!
The power of men lies within,
mysteriously hidden.
Those fearful poisons more powerfully
rob a man of his very self
which penetrate within,
and, doing no harm to the body,
bring savage wounds to the mind.

Boethius recites all this in short-line verses.

Sigismund. Although Boethius recites the deeds of Ulysses and his companions in such exalted style, still I doubt whether they are true, and whether the deeds themselves are true. But it is no cause for wonder if such things happened to pagans, who venerated idols and adored statues of demons, by which we believe the Devil held all the more power over them. But we, however, adore the God of heaven and believe in Christ, who freed us from the rule of the Devil, so I think such things cannot happen to us.

Conrad. Another case of this sort might be cited. For Apuleius tells (as Augustine relates) how he grew the ears of an ass, and when he took a potion he turned into an ass, while retaining a human soul.[27]

Sigismund. As I have already said, there is a difference between worshipers of idols and those who worship the God of heaven.

Conrad. Let us proceed, then, to those who adore the God of heaven, to show how similar things happen to them as well by the art of potion making.

Sigismund. Go ahead, then.

Conrad. In the history of Clement [of Rome],[28] it is told how the face of Faustinianus, the father of Saint Clement, and a friend of Saint Peter

27. See Julia Haig Gaisser, *The Fortunes of Apuleius and the Golden Ass: A Study in Transmission and Reception* (Princeton, NJ: Princeton University Press, 2008).

28. *SN*, bk. 2, chap. 110, col. 149; Pseudo-Clement of Rome, *Recognitions*, chaps. 52–72, and *Homilies*, chaps. 14–23, in *The Ante-Nicene Fathers: Translations of the Writings of the Fathers Down to AD 325*, vol. 8, ed. Alexander Roberts and James Donaldson, rev. A. Cleveland Coxe (Buffalo: Christian Literature Company, 1886), 205–11, 343–46; Jacobus de Voragine, *Golden Legend*, 2:328–29. The gist of the complex story: (a) Appion and Anubion are staying with Peter's enemy Simon Magus, and Faustinianus (Clement's father) comes with Peter's permission to greet them; (b) Simon Magus, fearing arrest as a magician, magically transforms Faustinianus's face into his own so that the authorities will arrest Faustinianus, but (c) he has Appion and Anubion anoint their own faces with the juice of a magic herb that will keep them from being deceived by the metamorphosis; (d) Faustinianus comes back to Clement and others, who are horrified to see the man who appears to be Simon, but (e) Peter recognizes Faustinianus by his voice and is not deceived; (f) Peter sends Faustinianus to Antioch so that, pretending to be Simon Magus, he can publicly renounce his previous slander of Peter; (g) Faustinianus, in the guise of Simon, tells the people of Antioch that an angel has come to him at night and rebuked him for his maligning of Peter, and so (h) the people turn back to Peter and against Simon; (i) Peter then causes Faustinianus to resume his own appearance. On the legends of Simon Magus see also *HMES*, vol. 1, chap. 17, pp. 400–427; and Alberto Ferreiro, *Simon Magus in Patristic, Medieval, and Early Modern Traditions* (Leiden: Brill, 2005).

the apostle, was changed by Simon the sorcerer. For that history tells that when the emperor had sent Cornelius the centurion to Antioch, to arrest magicians and sorcerers, Faustinianus asked from Saint Peter permission to go and greet Appian and Anubion. But when Faustinianus had turned to Simon the sorcerer, Simon showed Anubion and Appian how that night he wished to flee from Cornelius the centurion, because he had heard that this Cornelius wished to arrest him on the emperor's order, and so Simon planned to turn all the anger against Faustinianus. He said, "Have Faustinianus eat dinner with you, and I will concoct an unguent with which after dining he can anoint his face, causing him to seem to have my face. You, meanwhile, anoint your face with the juice of a certain plant so that you are not confused regarding the mutation. For I want him to be arrested by those who are seeking me, and I want grief to befall his sons when he leaves me and flees to Peter." And so the face of Faustinianus was changed so that no one but Peter knew him, in such a way that those who looked at Faustinianus thought they were seeing Simon Magus. And so the holy man was transformed by arts of bewitchment.

Sigismund. Perhaps at that time Faustinianus was a catechumen, and not yet baptized by Peter. Or perhaps God allowed this so that the deceit of Simon Magus might redound to the glory of Peter, as in fact happened.

Conrad. However it was that it was permitted, still from this story it is clear that his face was changed by bewitchment. So, too, in the story of Saint Peter it is said that when Simon the magician stood before the face of the emperor Nero his face was suddenly changed, so that he appeared sometimes older, sometimes more youthful. In the same story we also read that Simon the magician changed a goat into the form of a man—that of Simon himself. For it is reported that Simon said to Nero, "So that you may know, O excellent emperor, that I am the son of God, command me to be beheaded, and on the third day I will arise." Nero thus ordered the executioner to behead him, and when he thought he was beheading Simon, he beheaded a ram. Simon, gathering up the members of the ram, hid himself for three days, and on the third day he showed himself to Nero, saying, "Have my blood that was shed wiped away, for behold, I who was beheaded have arisen on the third day, as I promised." On seeing this, Nero was struck with amazement and thought that he was the son of God.[29]

Sigismund. Good doctor, what do you have to offer to the discussion?

Ulrich. The testimony of the greatest teachers, which lead in the same direction. For Saint Augustine argues in the [pseudonymous] book *On Spirit and Soul*,[30] "Human opinion says that by a certain art and by the power of demons men can be turned into wolves and livestock, and can be made to carry whatever things are required of them, and after they have carried out these works they return to themselves. [While they are transformed] they do not have the minds of beasts, but keep their rational and human minds. We should understand by this that demons do not create nature, but they can only bring it about that things seem to be as they are not." Note, then, that Augustine grants that they are able to do something of this sort.

Sigismund. But he adds that things seem to be as they are not.

Ulrich. We will speak further of this in our conclusions. Augustine also says in *The City of God*,[31] "What shall we say about the impostures of demons, except that we must 'flee from the depths of Babylon' [Isaiah 48:20], [. . .] for as we perceive that the power of demons is greater in regard to things below, the more firmly we should cling to the Mediator by whom we rise from the depths to the heights. [. . .] When I was in Italy I heard tales about a region in that land where they say innkeeper women imbued with these arts will give [potions] in cheese to travelers when they want and can do it, and they are at once turned into beasts of burden, and they carry whatever they are needed for, and after they have carried out these works they return to themselves. And yet they do not have bestial minds, but remain rational."

Sigismund. But Augustine is relating hearsay, for he says he had heard what certain people had to tell. Thus this statement of Augustine

29. "Acts of the Holy Apostles Peter and Paul," in *Ante-Nicene Fathers*, ed. Roberts and Donaldson, 482.

30. As given in *SN*, bk. 2, chap. 105, col. 146.

31. Augustine, *City of God*, bk. 18, chap. 18; cf. Dyson trans., 843.

proves nothing in this matter, for a witness speaking about hearsay does not furnish proof.

Ulrich. You speak wisely, but let us hear about things closer at hand. Vincent [of Beauvais] in his *Mirror of Nature*[32] addresses the issue: "The monk William of Malmesbury in his history tells that at the time of Peter Damian there were two old women along the public road whom Augustine calls inn keepers, that is women who take in wayfarers for a price. For an inn properly so called is a public lodging available for payment. These women, staying together in a cottage, steeped in every sort of bewitchment, changed a guest who arrived by himself into a horse or pig or ass and sold him to merchants. One day they received at their lodging a young man who with wild gestures was demanding food. When they had taken him in, they made him an ass, and they made quite a profit thereby, for the ass was able to detain passersby with his amazing comportment, for he would move in whatever way one of the old women commanded him, having lost his power of speech but not his understanding. The old women heaped up quite a bit of profit in this way. Hearing this, a rich neighbor bought the ass for quite a price. The old women told him he should keep the ass from entering water. But after the ass had been kept for a long time away from water, there finally came a point when their guard was less careful, and he threw himself into the nearest lake, and by thrashing about in it for a long time he lost the shape of an ass and regained his own form. When his keeper ran into him and asked if he had seen an ass, he said he himself was it. The servant went and told his master what had happened. The master reported it to Pope Leo, a man known for the greatest holiness. The old women were arrested and confessed the deed. The pope was in doubt, but Peter Damian, a most learned man, brought forth the example of Simon Magus, who caused Faustianus to be seen in Simon's own form." Take note, therefore, that Peter

32. *SN*, bk. 2, chap. 109, col. 148; David Rollo, *Glamorous Sorcery: Magic and Literacy in the High Middle Ages* (Minneapolis: University of Minnesota Press, 2000), 23–31; the story is also in Helinand's chronicle, in *PL*, vol. 212, col. 945.

Damian, a man and a teacher of great authority, explained to the pope that such things are possible.[33]

Sigismund. With stories and authorities like these you bring me to a point where I do not know how to respond.

Ulrich. Let us come back and say more about this matter at the end.

5. Whether they go to their assemblies riding on a stick or a wolf

Sigismund. I wonder further whether these accursed women can ride on a stick anointed with some unguent, or on a wolf or some other animal, and whether the Devil can carry them from place to place so they can drink and have feasts together and have sexual knowledge and delight with each other.

Ulrich. We would like to hear your own opinion, good archduke!

Sigismund. We know the Devil is an incorporeal spirit, without hands and feet or even wings, and he does not have spatial extension, so how would he be able to carry a man, who is corporeal?

Conrad. Perhaps spirits enter into and assume for themselves bodies fit for what they want to do, and then in those bodies they carry out what they wish. For in holy Scripture we read in the book of Daniel [14:35] that "an angel of the Lord seized Habakuk by the top of his head and carried him by the hair of his head, and put him down in Babylon." Although angels are spirits and do not have hands or feet, still it follows that an angel assumed a body by which he was able to hold and carry Habakuk's hair. So, too, in the Acts of the Apostles [8:39–40] we read that a spirit of the Lord seized Philip, and he was found in Azoth.

Sigismund. I grant that this could happen with good spirits and angels, who have greater power.

---

33. William of Malmesbury, *Chronicle of the Kings of England*, bk. 2, chap. 10, trans. J. A. Giles (London: Bell & Dalby, 1866), 180.

FIGURE 4 Male witch riding on a wolf, from *De laniis et phitonicis mulieribus*, sig. b ij[v].

Ulrich. So let us talk about evil spirits, and specifically the Devil. For in the legend of Saint James we read that the Devil bound Hermogenes and with his hands and feet fettered took him to Saint James.[34]

Conrad. I shall tell what happened in our own time, when we were still young and studying together in the humane sciences. Before many years had passed, I saw two men contending with each other in the provincial court of Constance. The accuser entered legal charges following old legal form against a peasant,[35] asserting that he was a sorcerer. He entered the accusation that this peasant, riding on a wolf, encountered the accuser, and upon this encounter the accuser suddenly became afflicted and weak in his members. He asked the sorcerer to restore his health to him, and the man promised to do so. So he went away, and for a while he kept silent about the matter, but because that peasant was said to have inflicted harm on other people with his bewitchment, at length the accuser charged him publicly in legal proceedings.

Sigismund. What did the peasant respond to this accusation?

Conrad. He denied it.

Sigismund. Was he subjected to torture?

Conrad. No.

Sigismund. How, then, could be convicted?

Conrad. By witnesses.

Sigismund. What did the witnesses depose?

---

34. Jacobus de Voragine, *Golden Legend*, 2:4.

35. Joseph Hansen, ed., *Quellen und Untersuchungen zur Geschichte des Hexenwahns und der Hexenverfolgung im Mittelalter* (1901; repr., Hildesheim: Olms, 1963), 570–71, gives archival evidence of a trial at Constance in 1458, in which one man (supported by six sworn witnesses) accused another of magical milk-theft and weather-magic; the trial, in which Ulrich Blaurer was spokesman for one of the principals, and Conrad Schatz for the other, led to the execution of the accused by burning. Molitoris's wording *accusator in forma iuris seni scribens* indicates that the trial followed the older accusatory procedure, in which one person took responsibility and liability for entering the accusation rather than denouncing the accused to a judge for inquisitorial examination.

Conrad. That he knew how to do such things.

Sigismund. But knowing things cannot be blamed, since as Aristotle says, "All men by nature desire to know."[36]

Conrad. But the witnesses added that the peasant not only knew how to do these things, but actually did them.

Sigismund. What basis did these witnesses have for their allegations?

Conrad. They claimed, under public oath, that this peasant sorcerer had harmed the witnesses themselves in their bodies and property.

Sigismund. Was the accused given a spokesman to defend him?

Ulrich. I was present at the trial, and I saw it carried out with serious and mature deliberation. I recall that both parties had men of great eloquence to introduce their causes.

Sigismund. Who were these?

Ulrich. They had as spokesmen the late Conrad Schatz, the father of our interlocutor [Conrad], and the late Ulrich Blarer, both magistrates in our city, and individuals worthy of renown as speakers.[37]

Sigismund. I knew them as judicious men.

Conrad. I saw the accused had been convicted in accordance with ordinary judicial form, on the testimony of the witnesses, and when he had been condemned I saw him burned.

Sigismund. The question under consideration involves another aspect, which is that women of this sort at times have gatherings in which they converse together and drink and have knowledge of each other.

---

36. Aristotle, *Metaphysica*, bk. A, chap. 1, 980a, trans. W. D. Ross, in *The Basic Works of Aristotle*, ed. Richard McKeon (New York: Random House, 1941), 689.

37. Reading *condisputantis* for *condisputantes.*

Conrad. Ordinary people proclaim that these things do happen,[38] and the women themselves confess to them, and they persist in their confessions.[39]

Sigismund. But does not the canon *Episcopi* say, "This, too, should not be passed over, that certain pernicious women, 'turned back to Satan' [I Timothy 5:15], seduced by illusions and phantasms of demons, believe and profess that they ride out with Diana the goddess of the pagans during the nighttime hours, and with Herodias, and with a countless multitude of women, riding on certain beasts, and in the dead of night they cross through many regions, obeying her commands as those of their mistress, and on certain nights they are called forth to her service. But would that they alone perished in their faithlessness, and did not lead many others with them to ruinous infidelity! For a countless multitude, deceived by this false opinion, believes this to be true, and by believing things that deviate from the true faith, they are ensnared in the error of the pagans."

Conrad. If, then, according to the words of the canon, they are deceived in their opinion, how does it come about that these women know men from other cities, claiming to have been with them in the assembly, and showing signs of their acquaintance, although they have never previously seen them or had dealings with them in their cities?

Ulrich. This issue may seem pressing, but we shall resolve it near the end of this treatise with an incident concerning Saint Germanus.

Sigismund. I think there is another matter to be examined.

---

38. *vulgus clamat*: an interesting assertion that something like belief in the Sabbath was rooted in popular belief.

39. The Latin here is *ipseque mulieres talia confitentur, et propinqua iuditia confessionis assignant*, which is somewhat unclear; the contemporary German translation gives *darzů so sy gefangen vnd peynlich gefragt werden so veriehen sy sŏllichs vnd melden auch vmbstend irer vergicht*, which says more explicitly that the accused confess under torture but afterward persist in their confession.

6. Whether the Devil can appear in the form of a man and have sex with these accursed women

Conrad. No one doubts that the Devil can appear in the form of a man. For in the legend of Saint Martin we read that when Martin passed through Milan he encountered the Devil in human form.[40] So, too, in the legend of Saint Anthony we read that the Devil appeared prostrate [before the saint] in the form of a black boy.[41] Again, in the legend of Saint Eligius we read that the Devil in the form of a beautiful woman spoke with him at his workshop.[42] In the gospel of Matthew [4:5] we read also regarding our Savior that the Devil took him and placed him on the pinnacle of the Temple, and so forth.[43] And so on this point I assert that the Devil could appear to men and enter into relations with them in human form. And we read that Plato [*sic*] had a domestic demon as a kind of servant.[44]

Sigismund. But what about the other part of the question, whether demons can sleep and have sex with these women?

Conrad. The women themselves confess that they have sex with incubi, who treat them in the manner of lovers.

Sigismund. Women with their vain opinions chatter about many things that they suppose to be true!

Conrad. But sometimes they persist in this confession even when they are being led to their execution and can having nothing to expect but their imminent death. Still, let us hear other evidence based on more authoritative sources. We read in the history of Saint Bernard that a

40. Jacobus de Voragine, *Golden Legend*, 2:293.
41. Ibid., 1:93. The demon had been tempting Anthony to fornication, but Anthony resisted, and the demon prostrated himself in submission to the saint.
42. Jean-Christophe Masmonteil, *Iconographie et culte de saint Éloi dans l'Occident médiéval* ([Châtillon-sur-Indre]: Rencontre avec le Patrimoine religieux, 2012), 68–72, and the plates on 46, 47, 57, and 73.

43. The phrase *de saluatore quoque nostro* clearly belongs with this sentence, not (as in JM-1997) with the preceding sentence.
44. David Berman, "Socrates' daimonion," in *Encyclopedia of Psychology and Religion*, ed. David A. Leeming, Kathryn Madden, and Stanton Marlan (New York: Springer, 2009), 858–61. Note that the *daimon* is that of Socrates, not Plato.

FIGURE 5 Witch embraced by a demon, from *De laniis et phitonicis mulieribus*, sig. b iv^v.

demon or incubus slept for several years with a woman, and even though he was also sleeping in the same bed the woman's husband was unaware of this abomination. At last the woman was brought to penitence and wished to send away and expel the incubus, but she could not. So she sought out Saint Bernard, who exorcised the demon with lighted candles, thus driving him away from the woman.[45] So, too, Saint Augustine in *The City of God* says that it is widely known, and many have experienced, or affirm that they have heard from others who experienced it, that "forest spirits and fauns, popularly known as incubi, have often acted immodestly with women, seeking and having sex with them."[46] Again, we read in the histories of Arthur king of Britain that such things have often happened.[47]

Sigismund. What response can be made, then, to the authority of Cassian, who says, "It should in no way be believed that spiritual natures can have carnal relations with women. For if this were at all possible, why is it that we never or scarcely at all see people born of their intercourse with women, without male seed? For it is quite certain that they [women] take great delight in their filthy lust, and no doubt they would prefer to carry it out on their own rather than with men, if that were at all possible."[48]

Ulrich. This authority leads us to another question.

7. Whether children can be born from intercourse of demons with women

Conrad. It is a widely held belief that children are born of such intercourse, and they are popularly called changelings, or in German idiom *wechselbalg*.[49] There is a story about an incuba Melusine, who is said

---

45. Jacobus de Voragine, *Golden Legend*, 2:105–6. The text says the saint "excommunicated" (*excommunicauit*) the spirit, meaning exorcised.

46. Augustine, *City of God*, bk. 15, chap. 23, Dyson trans., 681.

47. *SN*, bk. 2, chap. 127, col. 157.

48. This passage is misogynist in an oddly contorted way. Compare the translation in John Cassian, *The Conferences*, book 8, chap. 21, trans. Boniface Ramsey (New York: Paulist, 1997), 304.

49. *HDA*, 9:855–60.

to have been attached to a certain count, and several children were born to her, but the story has it that each of them was marked by some monstrous feature: one had three eyes, while another had the teeth of a wild boar.[50]

Sigismund. A fable like this, from some unestablished author, carries no credibility.

Conrad. According to Vincent [of Beauvais] in the *Liber historialis*, "King Vortigern took counsel with wise men about what he should do for his defense, and when he had received their advice he had workmen brought together to construct a well-fortified tower. But what they built sank into the earth, so the king was persuaded to seek out a man without a father and ordered the rocks and mortar sprinkled with his blood, in the expectation that the mortar would hold fast when this was done. A young man was thus found, named Merlin,[51] who was summoned before the king along with his mother, and she affirmed that she had conceived him by a spirit in the form of a man. Merlin disclosed many mysteries and predicted many future things. He revealed that beneath the foundation there was a lake, and under the lake two dragons lay, a red one signifying the British people, and a white one signifying the Saxons. And he predicted which [of them] would conquer the other in their conflict, and said that Aurelius Ambrosius would reign when Hengist was conquered and Vortigern was burned."[52] From this history, then, you have the case of Merlin

50. See Jean d'Arras, *Melusine: or, The Noble History of Lusignan*, trans. Donald Maddox and Sara Sturm-Maddox (University Park: Pennsylvania State University Press, 2012); Donald Maddox and Sara Sturm-Maddox, eds., *Melusine of Lusignan: Founding Fiction in Late Medieval France* (Athens: University of Georgia Press, 1996).

51. Peter Goodrich, ed., *The Romance of Merlin: An Anthology* (New York: Garland, 1990); Silvia Brugger-Hackett, *Merlin in der*

europäischen Literatur des Mittelalters (Stuttgart: Helfant, 1991); Anne Berthelot, "L'héritage de Merlin," in *Zauberer und Hexen in der Kultur des Mittelalters*, ed. Danielle Buschinger and Wolfgang Spiewok (Greifswald: Reineke-Verlag, 1994), 1–10; Stephen Knight, *Merlin: Knowledge and Power Through the Ages* (Ithaca, NY: Cornell University Press, 2009); Nikolai Tolstoy, *The Quest for Merlin* (Boston: Little, Brown, 1985).

52. *SH*, bk. 20, chap. 30, p. 791.

diabolically born of an incubus. Saint Augustine and other teachers also make mention of this Merlin.[53]

Sigismund. What then do the teachers think about Merlin?

Ulrich. Near the end of this treatise that will be set forth more fully. Let us for now proceed to the point about incubi. The book of Genesis [6:4] says, "And there were giants on the earth in those days, for after the sons of God went in to the daughters of men, they gave birth; they are the mighty men of that age, and men of renown." The *Glossa ordinaria* on that text says, "It is not unbelievable that such men were procreated by humans, not by angels or by demons who acted immodestly with women, because after the flood the bodies not only of men but also of women were of unbelievable size."[54]

Sigismund. This gloss would be strange, if the Devil could beget children.

Ulrich. Josephus, the noble prince of the Jews, a man learned in many matters, whom even Jerome mentions with praise, wrote about this passage and asserts that they were born of intercourse of incubi spirits with women.[55]

Conrad. Let me cite more recent histories. Geoffrey of Auxerre writes, as Vincent tells in the third book *On Nature*, that "an ecclesiastical official who lived for a time in the kingdom of Sicily, with a sister of the duke of Burgundy, who was betrothed to King Roger of Sicily, gained certain knowledge there about something that had happened. A vigorous young man, skilled in the art of swimming, was bathing in the sea at dusk by the light of the moon, and he grabbed by the hair a woman swimming after him, as if she were one of his companions wishing to push him down into the water, but when he spoke to her

53. Augustine, *City of God*, bk. 15, chap. 23, trans. Dyson, 680–85, does not in fact mention Merlin.

54. *Glossa ordinaria*, gloss on Genesis 6:2, ascribed to Walafridus Strabo in his *Opera omnia*, in *PL*, vol. 113, col. 104.

55. Jerome, Letter 70, in Saint Jerome, *Letters and Select Works*, 150; but see Flavius Josephus, *Judean Antiquities: Translation and Commentary*, trans. Louis H. Feldman (Leiden: Brill, 2000), bk. 1, para. 174, and n. 553.

he was unable to get a single word from her, so he covered her with a mantle, took her home, and in the course of time took her solemnly as his wife. On one occasion a companion reprimanded him for taking to himself a phantom woman. He grew fearful, snatched a sword, and in the sight of the woman threatened the child he had begotten by her, saying he would kill the child unless she spoke and told him where she was from. 'Alas for poor you!' she said. 'By forcing my to speak you lose a wife who is good for you.[56] I would have stayed with you, and things would have gone well for you, if you had allowed me to maintain the silence enjoined for me. But now you will see me no longer.' And at once she vanished. The boy grew up, and began to spend time at the seashore. One day that phantom woman came, and in the sight of many she snatched the child as he ran about in the waves. If he had been a real child, the sea should have cast him back onto the shore."[57]

Sigismund. So was the boy real, or was he a phantom?

Conrad. From the history we find that this boy ate, drank, walked about, and was brought up over many years.

Ulrich. We will explain toward the end how Merlin and this boy should be understood. For now, meanwhile, let us proceed to other cases of this sort.

Sigismund. Go on, then.

Conrad. Helinand in his fourth book, which Vincent cites, likewise tells a story in these words: "In the diocese of Cologne there is a renowned and immense palace that towers over the Rhine River, which is called Juvamen. Once, when many princes were gathered there, a little ship came up unexpectedly, drawn by a swan to which it was bound with a silver chain around its neck. A newcomer knight, unknown to all, disembarked, and the swan took the ship back. The knight later took a wife and had children. But at length, as he was residing in that palace, he saw the swan approaching with the little

---

56. The contemporary German says *du verliirest ain gütte haußfrawen.*

57. *SN*, bk. 2, chap. 126, cols. 156–67.

ship on the chain, and at once he boarded the ship and was no more seen. But his offspring continues to this very day."[58]

Sigismund. Although the authors of these histories are serious men, it would be no less serious to believe such things really happened, and if they indeed happened to fathom how they should be understood. But because you say you want to resolve such doubts as best you can at the end [of this work], let me proceed to the next question.

8. Whether witches are able to foretell future things and to reveal the secret counsels of princes

Conrad. We have heard how Merlin predicted many future things, which, as the histories make clear, came to pass. And was not Balaam a fortune-teller, as Scripture attests? And yet he predicted many future things [Numbers 22–24]. And did not the Devil in the form of Samuel, conjured forth by the pythoness, predict that Saul and all his family would fall in battle, as came to pass, as is said in the first book of Kings? For Saul fell in battle, and Jonathan his son, and his family, and they died [I Kings 28:8–31:2].

Sigismund. But is it not God alone who knows the future and observes secrets, he being the prime cause and prime mover of all things?

Ulrich. Indeed he is, yet the Devil can predict future things. For we see that the physicians and astrologers and other wise men, too, often prognosticate the future.

Sigismund. Although they predict the future, still it is not necessary that things will turn out as they have said, so in predicting the future they do not draw necessary conclusions.

---

58. Ibid., bk. 2, chap. 127, col. 157. This is one of the early versions of the Swan Knight story; see Robert Jaffray, *The Two Knights of the Swan, Lohengrin and Helyas: A Study of the Legend of the Swan-Knight, with Special Reference to Its Most Important Developments* (New York: Putnam, 1910), 8.

Ulrich. Your argument is quite right, O most worthy lord prince, because all things are in the power of God, and he takes counsel from none but himself.

Sigismund. I would like to know, then, how the Devil can foretell the future.

Ulrich. Listen to the words of Saint Augustine, given in the *Decretum*, chapter *Sciendum*: "It should be known that it is the nature of demons that the senses of an aerial body easily excel the senses of earthly bodies, and in their quickness, too, on account of the superior mobility of an aerial body, they incomparably surpass not only the running of any men or beasts but also the flight of birds. And by these two qualities found in an aerial body, namely, keenness of sense and rapidity of motion, they can declare or report many things they have discerned in advance, causing wonderment among men with their sluggish earthly senses. Because their life extends over such a long time, the demons also have far greater experience than humans can have in their brief lifetime. And by these capacities allotted to the nature of an aerial body, the demons not only predict many future things but also carry out many things that humans cannot say or do, causing men to think they are worthy of the service and divine honors they render to them, incited especially by the vice of curiosity, for the sake of false and earthly happiness and temporal preeminence. [. . .] Now because the question at hand is about divination by demons, it should first be known that the things they predict are often the very things they themselves are about to do. For they frequently receive power to inflict illnesses and to render the air itself unhealthy with corruption, and to urge perverse people and lovers of earthly conveniences to commit offenses, when their behavior gives them confidence that they will consent to such persuasion. They persuade in wondrous and invisible ways, entering into people's bodies unawares by means of their subtlety, and interposing themselves in people's thoughts by notions of the imagination,[59] whether in sleep or awake.

---

59. Augustine's text reads *imaginaria visa* (things seen in the imagination); Molitoris in the printed text has *iussa* (things commanded or bidden).

Sometimes they predict things they do not do, but they know in advance by natural signs that cannot come within the scope of human senses. The physician foresees things that a person ignorant of his art cannot foresee, yet he should not be thought divine on that account. What wonder is it, then, if, like the physician who foresees good or ill future health by the disturbed or weakened condition of the human body, so, too, the demons foresee future storms that are unknown to us but known to them by the condition of the air? Sometimes, too, people's inclinations are expressed not only in words but by bodily signs that reveal thoughts in the mind, and [the demons] can easily foretell many future things on this basis which seem wondrous to those who do not know of these connections."[60]

Sigismund. Should such things then be believed?

Ulrich. No, indeed!

Sigismund. Why?

Ulrich. Because the demons, too, are sometimes deceived, and they also dupe and deceive humans.

Sigismund. Give an example of how they are deceived.

Ulrich. We read in the legend of Saints Simon and Jude that when Wardach, the general of the king of the Babylonians, wished to go into war against the king of the Indians, he consulted magicians and fortune-tellers to receive replies about the outcome of the war from idols and demons, and they foretold that a great war would take place, and those fighting on both sides would be killed. When Wardach had heard this he fell into sadness. The apostles Simon and Jude, however, were aroused to laughter. The general said, "Fear has befallen me, and here you laugh!" The apostles said, "Set your fear aside—peace has entered this province along with us. Leave off your departure today, and tomorrow those you have sent ahead will come at the third hour along with legates from the Indians, who will make a solid pact, gladly

---

60. *Decretum*, pt. 2, case 26, qu. 3, chap. 2, in *CIC*, vol. 1, cols. 1025–26, taken from Augustine's *De divinatione demonum*, chap. 3 and 5. Compare Brown's translation in "The Divination of Demons," chaps. 3 and 5, pp. 426–27 and 430.

agreeing to accept peace on whatsoever conditions." The fortune-tellers now in turn laughed, saying to the general, "Lord, do not believe those lying men, these unknown strangers, who say such things so that the messengers will not be detained. The gods who never deceive have given you their response, that you should be cautious and appre-hensive." In short, the next day messengers came who had been sent, and announced that things were exactly as the apostles had said.[61] Note that the demons were false and foretold lies, and no doubt these demons if they could, and if they truly had knowledge, would willingly have given true responses, since that lie worked against the demons' own interests. But because they did not know the future, they deceived themselves. Thus you have a case in which the demons deceive them-selves. But one should note that when these demons doubt about the outcome of what they predict, they make for uncertainty about how to proceed.[62] As Augustine says in the same chapter *Sciendum*, "But lest the weight of authority should be lost among those who worship them, they do this so that the blame may be assigned to their inter-preters who make conjectures about their signs when they themselves have been deceived or lie."[63]

Sigismund. Give an example.

Ulrich. We read about a general who, planning to fight against the Romans, consulted his gods—meaning his demons and fortune-tellers—about the victory. They did not know the outcome of the war, but wishing to give some response lest they be thought not to know the future, they said, "You can count on seeing a victory when you fight the Romans."[64] The wording can be construed more than one

---

61. Jacobus de Voragine, *Golden Legend*, 2:262–63, but in this edition the name Wardach is not given.

62. *Sed istud notandum est quod cum ipsi demones dubitant de euentu eorum que predicant, quid igitur faci-unt eum dubitant.* The contemporary German version is *Doch ist das auch zů mercken, so die bößen geist vnderweilen zweiflen wie es ergon solle, daz si dann künftig vorsagen wöllen, vnd damit man versteen mug wie sy ym thüen.*

63. *Decretum*, pt. 2, case 26, qu. 3, chap. 2, in *CIC*, vol. 1, cols. 1025–26.

64. Compare Cicero, *De divinati-one*, bk. 2, chap. 56, in Cicero, *De senectute, De amicitia, De divinatione*, trans. William Armistead Falconer (London: Heinemann; New York: Putnam, 1923), 500–501, on Apollo's oracular declaration to Pyrrhus. Cicero comments, in part, that the story must be bunk because Apollo spoke no Latin.

way, so that if the duke himself conquered this would be consistent with the response, but if he was conquered by the Romans, the demons could not be charged with giving false response.[65] They are accustomed to give responses in this way, with ambiguous obscurity. So, too, they often deceive intentionally and tell lies, because they are full of envy and rejoice when they bring people into error and dupe them. And so it is dangerous to believe in them, because a person does not know when they are deceived or meaning to deceive us, as is their custom. This is how things are, gracious prince, when they are able to know secrets and predict the future. And one should not put trust in their statements, because there is no truth in them.

Sigismund. We have now heard enough on this side and that in response to our doubts. Our mind seeks now a final solution to the issues that have been raised, so please let me know how you think these issues are to be resolved.

PART II

Ulrich. What doubts, then, do you wish to have settled?

Question 1 resumed. Whether demons can arouse hail and thunderstorms

Sigismund. [The first question is] whether demons and humans with the aid of demons can disturb the air and arouse hailstorms to damage the earth and people and cause illnesses, and make people sterile.

Ulrich. What I say is that they cannot do so, except when and to whom and insofar as God allows them, to manifest his majesty.

---

65. The response was an accusative with the infinitive, where the infinitive governs another accusative: *romanos te vincere certum habe*, which could be read "be certain that you will conquer the Romans" (taking the accusative *romanos* as the object of *vincere*) or "be certain that the Romans will conquer you" (reading the accusative *te* as the object of that infinitive). Falconer's translation has Apollo saying to Pyrrhus, "That you the Roman army will defeat."

FIGURE 6 Witches at a cauldron, performing weather magic, from *De laniis et phitonicis mulieribus*, sig. c iʳ.

Sigismund. On what do you base this conclusion?

Ulrich. On the considerations raised above. Furthermore, John of Damascus says, "Demons do not have powers against anyone unless they are granted by God," as happened with God's permission in the case of Job [1] and in that of the pigs [Matthew 8]. And they have such power, and are transformed and transfigured into whatever figure they wish, according to the imagination, which is to say by a phantasm.[66] Likewise Gregory says in his *Dialogues*, "Without the permission of almighty God, a malign spirit has no power against a human, and he could not even pass into the pigs without [divine] permission."[67]

Sigismund. What does it mean that he could not pass into pigs?

Ulrich. We read in the gospel that when Christ had cured a demoniac,[68] and had cast many legions of demons out of him, the demons asked permission from the Lord that they might enter pigs, and when it was granted they entered the pigs and rushed into the sea [Matthew 8:28–34, Mark 5:1–20, Luke 8:26–29]. Note that the demons did not dare enter the pigs and molest them until first they had obtained permission from God.

Sigismund. I know that when God gave them permission then they were able to cause harm.

Ulrich. You understand correctly. Thus Jerome says about Psalm 34, "The Psalm speaks thus about certain persons: 'Let there be [. . .] an angel of the Lord tormenting them,' that is to say a devil, or evil spirit, because they Lord created him, and has him in his power."[69] You can see from this that God often concedes to the Devil that he may torment humans. So, too, Saint Augustine says in his work *On the Divination of Demons*, "They often receive power to inflict illnesses and

66. John of Damascus, *An Exact Exposition of the Orthodox Faith*, bk. 2, chap. 4, in Saint John of Damascus, *Writings*, trans. Frederic H. Chase, Jr. (New York: Fathers of the Church, 1958), 209–10.

67. Gregory the Great, *Dialogues*, bk. 3, chap. 21, trans. Odo John Zimmerman (New York: Fathers of the Church, 1959), 153.

68. Reading *demoniacum* for *demonia cum*.

69. Jerome, *Breviarium in Psalmos*, Psalm 34[:6], in *PL*, vol. 26, col. 980.

render the air unhealthy with corruption, and they induce the perverse [. . .] to commit evil deeds."[70] And Saint Augustine says in his treatise *On the Trinity*, "By the ineffable power of God, there are certain things that the evil angels could do if they were allowed, but they cannot do them because they are not allowed."[71]

Sigismund. But when God permits the demons to do such things, can they do as much as they wish, according to their own liking?

Ulrich. No, but only so far as is allowed them. Thus Augustine says in the same passage of *On the Trinity*, "Therefore they cannot [do something] because they are not permitted," and he adds, "nor is there any other reason why the magi were unable to make stinging insects, when they made frogs and serpents, except that the rule of God preventing them was greater, through the Holy Spirit, as the magi themselves acknowledged when they said, 'This is the finger of God,'" as it says in Exodus [8:19]. And so John Chrysostom says in his commentary on Matthew, "The Devil does not tempt people as much as he wishes, because left to himself he would never desist from temptation, nor does he have any other undertaking, for he does not eat or sleep or do anything else but tempt, deceive, and bring ruin. This is his food [cf. Leviticus 22:7]."[72] Note, then, what John Chrysostom says, "He does not tempt . . . as much as he wishes." So, too, Peter Lombard in his *Sentences*, says, "The magic arts are worked by the knowledge and power of demons, but their power and knowledge are given by God, either to deceive the deceivers (like the Egyptians, and in particular the magi, that by their working with spirits they might seem worthy of wonder, when in God's truth they were worthy of condemnation), or as a warning to the faithful (lest they desire to do anything of the sort, thinking of it as something grand), or to exercise, test, and manifest the patience of the righteous. [. . .] And it should not be thought that the matter of visible things serves

---

70. *Divination of Demons*, trans. Brown, chap. 5, p. 430.

71. Saint Augustine, *The Trinity*, bk. 3, chap. 9; cf. the translation by Stephen McKenna (Washington, DC: Catholic University of America Press, 1963), 113;

the Latin is slightly inexact in Molitoris's rendering.

72. See UM-1997, 121n75; also cf. Gregory the Great's *Moralia in Iob*, bk. 33, chap. 16, in *PL*, vol. 76, col. 694.

the will of the demons, but rather it serves God, by whom this power is given."[73]

Sigismund. Now, if it were possible to ascertain it, I would like to know under what conditions the glorious God grants and permits it to demons to harm the earth and humans, and to disrupt the air and the waters.

Ulrich. That is a weighty question, for who knows the will of God? The apostle Paul in the epistle to the Romans [11:33–35] cries out, "O the depth of the riches of the wisdom and knowledge of God! How incomprehensible are the judgments of God and unsearchable his ways. For who has known the mind of the Lord, or who has been his counselor, or has given first to him and will be repaid by him?"

Sigismund. Although it is not allowed to investigate all the mysteries of God, still let us speak as much as is allowed to us from on high by grace.

Ulrich. I maintain, then, that frequently perturbation of the air, storms, thunder, and other such phenomena can occur without the ministry of demons, from the natural disposition of things and from the motion of the planets, as God's goodness allows the stars to run their courses. The philosophers have much to say about these causes, as Aristotle writes in his book *On Meteorology*.[74]

Sigismund. There is no doubt that such things can occur by natural motion. But the question is when the Devil is given the power to do these things.

Ulrich. The most merciful Lord God, who disposes all things with his gracious providence for the benefit of humans, sometimes allows such things as a punishment for the correction of sinners, sometimes as a temptation for the increase of merits, sometimes as a portent giving occasion for later thanksgiving.

73. Magister Petrus Lombardus, *Sententiae in IV libris distinctae*, bk. 2, dist. 7, chap. 6, in vol. 1, pt. 2, 3rd ed. (Grottaferrata: Collegium S. Bonaventurae ad Claras Aquas, 1971), 362, but Peter Lombard is here quoting Saint

Augustine, *The Trinity*, bk. 3, chap. 7; cf. the translation by McKenna, 107–8. Again, the text is quoted in Molitoris with some imprecision.

74. Also cited by Hartlieb, chap. 77.

Sigismund. How then does God punish sins in this way?

Ulrich. Sometimes with our knowledge and sometimes without.

Sigismund. How does this happen with our knowledge?

Ulrich. When people are punished manifestly, they knowingly recognize themselves as punished for their sins. Thus in the destruction of Sodom and Gomorra men realized that they were punished for their sins [Genesis 19:1–29]. So, too, when the earth swallowed up Abyron and Dathan in the sight of all [Numbers 16:1–50, esp. 27b–33].

Sigismund. And how does it happen without their knowledge?

Ulrich. This point is relevant to the present subject. Without their knowledge, God sometimes punishes people's sin by an angel, sometimes by a human, and sometimes by the Devil.

Sigismund. Give an example of how he has carried out correction by means of an angel.

Ulrich. It is said in Isaiah that when Sennacherib had come to besiege Jerusalem an angel of the Lord went out and struck 185,000 men in his camp, showing that God punished the pride of the Assyrians by his angel, killing so many thousands of them [Isaiah 37:36–38; cf. II Kings 19:35–37, II Chronicles 32:20–22]. So, too, he punished the hardness of Pharaoh and the Egyptians by an angel, killing all the firstborn of Egypt [Exodus 12:29].

Sigismund. Then how does he punish by means of humans?

Ulrich. You can find many examples in the canon *Remittuntur*:[75] the people of the Hebrews were punished by Nebuchadnezzar [II Kings 25], and by Antiochus [I Maccabees 1–6], and by Titus and Vespasian.[76] The same text says that Assur, that is Sennacherib, was the rod of the Lord's wrath, because God's justice disposed him to chastise countless multitudes [Isaiah 10:5]. So, too, Attila the king of the Huns

---

75. *Decretum*, pt. 2, case 23, qu. 5, chap. 49, in *CIC*, vol. 1, cols. 945–47.

76. Flavius Josephus, *Wars of the Jews*, bk. 3, chap. 10, and bk. 5, chaps.

2–3, in *The Works of Flavius Josephus*, trans. William Whitson, rev. Samuel Burder, vol. 1 (New York: American Book Exchange, 1880), 310–14, 359–65.

called himself the Scourge of God.[77] Again, the text adds, "But Assur did not know, because, puffed up with pride, he ascribed the victory he had won not to divine power but to his own powers. Thus the Lord speaks against his pride, 'Does the saw pride itself in the face of him who saws, or is the axe exalted in the face of him who cuts with it?' [cf. Isaiah 10:15]." This passage is in the same canon *Remittuntur*.

Sigismund. Now for the third category, how does he punish by means of the Devil?

Ulrich. That brings us to the subject at hand. For we heard the prophet saying above in the Psalm, "Let there be [. . .] an angel of the Lord"— that is to say, a devil—"pursuing them" [Psalms 35:6, 34:6 in the Vulgate], along with other authorities that have been cited. And thus sinners are sometimes afflicted in body, sometimes in their goods. We see that energumens, demoniacs, and obsessed people are tortured in body. So, too, we see people contract many infirmities on account of sins. And thus the text in the chapter *Cum infirmitas* says, "Since bodily infirmity sometimes comes from sin, as the Lord said to the sick man whom he had healed, 'Go and sin no more, lest something worse happen [to you]' [John 5:14, cf. 8:11], in the present decree we ordain and command physicians of the body that when they are called to the sick they should before all else admonish them and lead them to summon physicians of souls, so that after provision for spiritual remedy has been made, the remedy of bodily medicine may have more salutary effect, since when the cause ceases the effect also ceases."[78] Take for example Nebuchadnezzar, king of the Babylonians, who for the sin of pride was beset with afflictions to mind and body, walked about on all fours, thought he was an ox, and is said to have eaten grass.[79] The text in the chapter *Si per sortiarias*, "If by sorceries and arts of bewitchment," goes on, "with the permission of God's judg-

77. *SH*, bk. 16, chap. 15, p. 622.

78. Fourth Lateran Council, canon 22, in *Decrees of the Ecumenical Councils*, ed. and trans. Norman P. Tanner, 2 vols. (Washington, DC: Georgetown University Press, 1990), 1:245–46.

79. Ronald Herbert Sack, *Images of Nebuchadnezzar: The Emergence of* a *Legend*, 2nd ed. (Selinsgrove, PA: Susquehanna University Press, 2004); Penelope Reed Doob, *Nebuchadnezzar's Children: Conventions of Madness in Middle English Literature* (New Haven, CT: Yale University Press, 1974).

ment, which is mysterious but never unjust, and with the Devil's involvement, intercourse does not ensue."[80] Note that the canon specifies that by God's mysterious judgment, with the Devil's procurement, a man can be bewitched. And thus you can see that in inflicting punishments God uses the Devil as a minister.

Sigismund. How then do these bewitching women believe and claim that they themselves do such things as disturbing the air, arousing storms, and inflicting illnesses on people?

Ulrich. It is out of their foolishness that they believe they do such things, but they are deceived by their credulity.

Sigismund. How so?

Ulrich. Sometimes the Devil knows from the motion of the elements that there will be a change in the air and storms will come, which the Devil (as we have said above) is able to foresee more easily and quickly than a human. And sometimes by divine permission some plague and correction for sins is to fall on the earth by God's just judgment, and he [the Devil] is deputed by God's providence as the executor of this plague and correction, so that he knows in advance that this plague will occur. He then moves the minds of these bewitching women, urging them on, or moving them to vengeance by the ill will these sinful women bear toward their neighbors. And he leads them astray, as if teaching them the means for arousing such storms and disturbances of the air.

Sigismund. What does he teach them to do, and how does he instruct them, leading these women to provoke such harmful events and to carry them out by their bewitchment?

Ulrich. He counsels and teaches them to do something foolish and vain, which has no bearing on the outcome.

Sigismund. If he then teaches them to do something foolish, how does it come about that after these women follow these instructions storms do in fact occur, just as they intend?

80. *Decretum*, pt. 2, case 33, qu. 1, chap. 4, in *CIC*, vol. 1, col. 1150.

Ulrich. The Devil foresees from the course of nature and the elements that a plague will fall on the earth, or else he knows that by divine permission it will occur and that the power to cause it has been granted him, and thus he knows that the event is in any case going to happen. But these sinful women believe they cause such things by following the Devil's instruction. The Devil teaches them to take flint stones and cast them to the west behind their backs, or to sprinkle in the air the sand taken from flowing water, or to boil pigs' bristles in a pot, or to take logs or sticks and place them crosswise along river-banks, and to do some other such foolishness. And the Devil will specify the day and the hour when they should do these things. Believing these instructions of the Devil, these foolish women actually go out and do these and other such things. And when they have done all this, storms and hail and other damage will ensue, which the Devil already knew would happen at that time, as we have seen. But these sinful and foolish women believe the outcome was brought about by what they themselves did, although their actions cannot bring forth a single raindrop. These women then heap favor on the Devil, worshiping him and making offerings to him, and rendering sacrifices or suchlike to him. But who is so stupid as to believe that by such foolishness and by the silly operation of women the immense sphere of the atmosphere and the other elements could be moved so much as to arouse hail and thunderstorms?

Sigismund. What then do you say to the fact that we often see an entire land imperiled when not everyone in it has given offense?

Ulrich. Often the just perishes with the impious, and someone is punished on account of another. For in Genesis [19:24–25] we read that when Sodom and Gomorra were engulfed [in fire and brimstone] on account of sin, other cities perished along with them because of their proximity, such as Segor and Jegor, and yet these cities had not sinned. So, too, in II Kings we see that David had sinned before the Lord by numbering the people [of Israel], and because of the sin of a single person, David, a multitude of people, indeed many thousands of people, died [II Samuel 24:1–25 in modern Bibles]. But when we read that God struck such a great multitude of people on account of the sin of numbering committed by only one man, how much the more then will the Lord punish the people on account of greater sins such as heresy and blasphemy! And when such women—as the text in the canon *Episcopi* says—deny God, and give themselves to Satan, adoring the Devil, and offering sacrifices to him, who can doubt that an entire town in which such sinful women live and are tolerated will be more wretched and have cause to fear destruction when the divine majesty takes vengeance?

Sigismund. We see, then, a distinction of two ways in which the Devil knows of future storms: first from the motion of the stars and the natural disposition of things, and second in the case of God's punishment or correction of sinners. But what can we make of it when such harms befall upright and just persons?

Ulrich. Already above we have discussed other modes of divine permission: sometimes God grants permission for the temptation of the just, and sometimes for the augmentation of merit.

Sigismund. Show how that is so.

Ulrich. Was Job not a just man, giving praise to God, yet the Lord tempted him in his goods, his fields, his herds and flocks, and then also in his body, giving the Devil power to tempt him, even inflicting a grievous ulcer on him. And because in all this Job was found patient and humble, he had merit before God [Job 1–2]. Was not Saint Anthony the hermit a devout man, worthy of the Lord's love, and yet was he not often tempted by the Devil and struck so gravely that he nearly expired, and thus his merit was increased. You have read in his legend that "when Anthony was hiding in a tomb, a multitude of demons inflicted all sorts of torments on him, so that his attendant, coming from the village, found him nearly dead and carried him on his shoulders to the village inn, and when those living nearby heard of this they came and made funeral lamentation, but then in the middle of the night went to sleep. Anthony, suddenly reviving, called his attendant and had himself carried back to the tomb in silence. There, lying prostrate out of pain from the former wounds, with strength of spirit he challenged the demons to further conflict, and at once they came, changed into the forms of various beasts, and he was slashed by their teeth, their horns, and their claws. Suddenly a ray of light put the demons and the darkness to flight. Healed at once, understanding that Christ was present, he said, 'Where were you, good Jesus? Where were you, and why were you not present from the beginning to cure my wounds?' And a voice addressed him, saying, 'Anthony, I was here, but I waited to see your struggle, and now, because you fought manfully, I will make your name known throughout the world.'"[81] Vincent in his *Historiale* notes that Athanasius retells these things.[82] And it is said in [the epistle of] James [1:12], "Blessed is the man who suffers temptation, for when he has been tested he will receive a crown of life."

Sigismund. I have heard enough now about how these women's actions cannot cause tempests, hailstorms, or any other evils, which occur only from natural motion or by permission of God's goodness, which out of ineffable graciousness permits such things to occur by the ministry of devils, either as punishment or for merit. And so let us direct our attention to other questions.

Question 4 resumed. Whether sorcerers and witches can change themselves and other people with the aid of demons into the other forms, giving them different appearances, including that of animals

Ulrich. From the cases considered above it is clear that they can do so, but in appearance and by illusion

Sigismund. What do you mean by illusion?

Ulrich. The art of transforming forms in their outer appearance is called enchantment, as if it is done by enchanting people's eyes, as Isidore says in the *Etymologies*.[83] By enchanting the eyes, demons make people appear to be something different from what they are.

81. Compare the translation in Jacobus de Voragine, *Golden Legend*, 1:93–94.

82. *SH*, bk. 13, chap. 91, p. 536.

83. Isidore of Seville, *Etymologiae*, bk. 8, chap. 9, sect. 33, p. 183: "They are called illusions (*praestrigium*) because they dull (*praestringere*) the sharpness of one's eyes." The play on words is difficult to convey in translation.

And so someone seeing a human believes he is an ass or a wolf, and yet the individual retains his form, and it is our eyes that are deceived and by erroneous judgment fixed on a different form.[84] Thus Simon Magus enchanted the eyes of Nero and the executioner who, beheading a ram, thought he had beheaded Simon, being deceived through the agency of the Devil with enchantment of his eyes.[85] So, too, we read of the hermit Saint Macarius the Egyptian, as Vincent tells in his *Historical Book*, that a certain Egyptian was driven mad with love for another's wife but was unable to achieve the aim of his concupiscence because she was deeply in love with the husband of her youth.[86] So he sought out a sorcerer, asking him either to make her love him or to have her rejected by her own husband. Won over by many gifts, the magician used the accustomed craft of his art to make her appear as a mare. And so her husband, disturbed at seeing a mare lying in his bed, sighed and wept because, speaking to her, he could hear no response. He summoned priests, and showed them what had befallen her, but the cause of her misfortune remained a mystery. So he tied her up and led her off into the desert like a beast of burden. But when he approached the cell of Saint Macarius, the monks reproved him for coming to the monastery with a mare. "This was my wife," he said, "but she has been changed into a mare. It has been three days now that she has not taken any food." They had passed this report along to Saint Macarius, to whom God had already made the matter known, and he said, "You people are [as brutish as] horses, and you have the eyes of horses. For that is actually a woman, and it is only those deceived by the vanity of illusion who see her transfigured in that shape." He sprinkled her with holy water and said a prayer, and then all at once he made everyone see that she was a woman. He ordered nourishment brought for her, and he had her return home with her husband, saying, "She should never hold back from participation in the holy liturgy or from the Church's prayer, for she has suffered these things because for five weeks she

---

84. Latin: *et ad aliam spetiem erroneo iuditio deducuntur.*

85. "Acts of the Holy Apostles Peter and Paul," in *Ante-Nicene Fathers*, ed. Roberts and Donaldson, 482.

86. Latin: *illa virginitatis sue coniugem nimis amaret.* French: *l'epoux gardien de son honneur.* However, cf. Joel 1:8.

did not attend the divine liturgy." Take note here that not everyone' eyes were enchanted, because the eyes of Saint Macarius were not affected by enchantment.[87]

Sigismund. This story sheds much light on our subject.

Ulrich. Indeed, once I spoke about the same matter with the most reverend Lord Otto, the bishop of Constance, from the family of the counts of Sonnenberg,[88] who has knowledge of many things and great fondness for scholarly discussion. He cited this same story, and I was very much enlightened on this matter of illusion, on account of this lord bishop's authority and his diligent study. I am his humble servant and take refuge under the wings of his kindness.

Sigismund. I would like to hear about other ways one thing can appear as another to people's eyes.

Ulrich. Saving the judgment of those wiser than myself, I will add two or three considerations, according to what I have been able to put together with my meager learning but following the reasoning of Saint Thomas in his commentary on the *Sentences*,[89] and of other doctors. In one way, it seems to me, the Devil can delude our senses inwardly by moving the phantasms and likenesses of things existing in the imaginative power, making them pass over into the organs of the outer senses. This sometimes happens in dreams. For in dreams there is motion of phantasms, which pass to the organs of outward senses: to the tympanum, in which hearing is grounded, and the eye, in which vision occurs. And so it appears to us that we see or hear many things. It sometimes happens to us even when we are awake that we see many things, as when people suffer delirium or high fever. In a second way, when attention is forcefully turned to the phan-

---

87. *SH*, bk. 17, chap. 70, p. 679.

88. Otto IV of Sonnenberg, bishop of Constance (reigned 1474–91); see Franz Josef Worstbrock, "Otto von Sonnenberg," in *Verfasserlexikon: Die deutsche Literatur des Mittelalters*, 2nd ed., vol. 11 (Berlin: de Gruyter, 2004), cols. 1154–56.

89. Thomas Aquinas, *In 4 libros Sententiarum*, bk. 2, dist. 8, qu. 1, art. 5, in Saint Thomas Aquinas, *Opera omnia*, ed. Roberto Busa, vol. 1 (Stuttgart-Bad Cannstatt: Frommann-Holzboog, 1980), 147–48.

tasms, this causes a likeness of a thing to appear as the thing itself. Thus Saint Augustine says that when a man thinks about the image of a woman with such forceful attention it can seem to him even when he is awake that he is having carnal relations with her.[90] Since a demon is not unaware of these processes, it seems to me that a demon can dispose the sense organs in such a way that one thing will appear as another. So, too, from the abundance of choleric humor it seems to the taste that all things are bitter, even though they may be sweet, and from the congestion of sanguine humor or fiery vapor in the eyes it seems to us that the things we see outside us are red. Secondly I propose that the Devil can dispose the medium [of sensation] in such a way that one thing appears as another. Thus, according to Saint Bonaventure it sometimes happens that by means of a candle made by [magic] art pieces of straw appear to be serpents, and many experiments of this sort are carried out by illusionists.[91] And since the Devil is the master of illusionists, no one can doubt that the Devil is able to do such things yet more subtly. And sometimes it is not the thing itself but the likeness and form of a thing that is seen. Thus, according to Saint Augustine's commentary,[92] Saint Peter saw a vessel lowered from heaven to earth in which there were all four-footed creatures, serpents of the earth, and birds of the sky, as is said in the Acts of the Apostles [10:10b–12], but these things were merely images, not bodily realities. By the same kind of vision, Benedict saw the entire world. For his legend tells that the whole world came before his eyes as if gathered in a single ray of sunlight, when it was the images of things that appeared.[93] From all this we are led on, then, to other questions.

90. Perhaps taken from *SN*, bk. 26, chap. 66, col. 1879.

91. Bonaventure, *Commentaria in quatuor libros sententiarum Magistri Petri Lombardi*, bk. 2, dist. 8, pt. 2, art. unicus, qu. 3, conclusio, in *Opera omnia*, ed. Collegium a S. Bonaventura, vol. 2 (Quaracchi: Collegium S. Bonaventurae, 1885), 229.

92. Saint Augustine, *The Literal Meaning of Genesis*, bk. 12, chap. 11, para. 24, trans. John Hammond Taylor (New York: Newman Press, 1982), 475–76.

93. Jacobus de Voragine, *Golden Legend*, 1:193.

Question 5 resumed. Whether they come to their assemblies on wolves or anointed sticks and eat and drink together, and speak together, and recognize each other

Sigismund. I would be pleased to hear your opinion on this question, also.

Ulrich. From what has been said you know how both in sleep and in waking life the impression of imagined things can sometimes be so strong that a person believes he really sees and does this or that. You have also heard how the Devil sometimes enchants the eyes and the other senses of people, so that they claim they have done this or that. But so that you can understand my point more fully, let me tell a story from the legend of Saint Germanus.[94] It is said that this saint was a guest one night in a house, and after dinner the table was again set. Saint Germanus wondered at this, and asked his hosts for whom the table was newly set, and they said they were setting it for the good men and women who came at night. That night, therefore, Saint Germanus determined to remain awake. He saw a multitude of demons come to the table in the forms of men and women. Commanding them not to depart, he woke everyone in the household and asked if they recognized those persons, and they all said they were men and women from the neighborhood. So he sent to the houses of all the neighbors, and they were found in their beds. Saint Germanus then adjured the demons, and they acknowledged that they were malign spirits who deluded people in this way. You see, then, that spirits can show themselves in the place of other individuals, in such a way that people think such images are the true persons. And thus from this story you have an example of how a person at one and the same time can be in one place and yet appear by means of a spirit in another place, just as those persons during the night were at home and in their beds, at the same time their images appeared by diabolical illusion having dinner in the house of the host. So, too, it is said of Simon Magus, in the legend of Saint Peter, that Simon was at one and the same time inside meeting with Nero while he was outside speak-

94. Ibid., 2:28.

FIGURE 7 Witches gathered for a meal, from *De laniis et phitonicis mulieribus*, sig. d iʳ.

ing with the people—that is, his image spoke outside with the people through the agency of the Devil.[95] The same can take place involving good spirits and angels, for we read that it appeared to Saint Ambrose that [he was celebrating mass in Milan and went into a trance, in which] he celebrated the funeral service of Saint Martin in the city of Tours. For he said [on being aroused], "I was officiating at the funeral rite, but when you aroused me I was not able to say the final prayer." And indeed it was found to be as he said, even though at that time Ambrose was in the city of Milan, which is several days' journey from Tours.[96] And according to Giles [of Rome] in a quodlibet of his, it is said that a good angel in the form of Saint Ambrose was in the city of Tours, while Saint Ambrose was physically in the city of Milan all along.[97]

Sigismund. What conclusion is this discourse leading up to?

Ulrich. What it shows is that people often think they see other people present in some place but what they actually see are images brought forth by either a good or an evil spirit.

Sigismund. But what about the case of pythonic women who believe they go to another location yet remain in their homes?

Ulrich. You have already heard examples in which a person believes he is in some location where he is not. Thus the text of the canon *Episcopi* speaks well in saying, "This, too, should not be passed over, that certain pernicious women, 'turned back to Satan' [I Timothy 5:15], seduced by illusions and phantasms of demons, believe and profess that they ride out with Diana the goddess of the pagans during the nighttime hours, and with Herodias, and with a countless multitude of women, riding on certain beasts, and in the dead of night they cross through many regions, obeying her commands as those of their mistress, and on certain nights they are called forth to her service. But

95. Perhaps referring to an incident in "Acts of the Holy Apostles Peter and Paul," in *Ante-Nicene Fathers*, ed. Roberts and Donaldson, 481.

96. Jacobus de Voragine, *Golden Legend*, 2:299.

97. Aegidius Columnae Romanus, *Quodlibeta*, quodlibet 1, membrum 1, qu. 1 (Louvain: Hieronymus Nempaeus, 1646), 2–4.

would that they alone perished in their faithlessness, and did not lead many others with them to ruinous infidelity! For a countless multitude, deceived by this false opinion, believes this to be true, and by believing things that deviate from the true faith."

Sigismund. But other people can simply ride and walk from place to place, both night and day, can't they? So what keeps these women from doing that?

Ulrich. Certainly I do not deny that women of this kind are able both to ride and to walk, going on asses, horses, oxen, or camels, or whatever, just like other people and in the manner of others, according to the natural course of things. But we are speaking about women who exceed the ordinary mode of humans, which prescribes that they cannot travel ten or twenty miles in one hour.

Sigismund. If then they do not go from place to place and participate at their assemblies, as the above text says, how does it come about that they know people who live in other cities, whom they never before saw?

Ulrich. The solution is clear from what has been said: they experience imaginary impressions or representation of phantasms brought about by the Devil's agency, but they believe they have experienced with their senses things physically present.

Sigismund. We are satisfied with the discussion on these matters. Let us now ask about one final question.

Questions 6–7 resumed. Whether the Devil can mingle with these women, lying with them in the form of a man, and whether from such coition children can be born

Ulrich. We have already brought forward a full range of authorities and rational arguments, and also exempla and stories enough to resolve this matter. I propose that a human cannot be procreated from an incubus and a woman. Nor has there ever been a human born of a spirit and a woman, apart from the Savior, our Lord Jesus Christ, who in the mercy of God the Father most high deigned to be born into the world by the Holy Spirit from the most glorious virgin Mary without the participation of a man. Far be it, then, I say, that a human should be born of a spirit and an accursed woman without a man. Nor is an obstacle that in the comedy of the poet Plautus about Amphitryon we read that Hercules was born of the god Jove and Alcmena, the wife of Amphitryon, and is thus called *Medius Fidius*, as if to say "middle son," because this fable of the poets is merely an impious fiction.[98]

Sigismund. What then do you say in response to what is said in the gloss on Genesis 1, where it is said that there were giants born of such coition?

Ulrich. I say the gloss speaks in a speculative and not a definitive manner.

Sigismund. But how do you explain the text that says giants were born thereby?

Ulrich. I say that "at that time there arose giants," that is to say, powerful and eminent men who, because of their power and magnanimity, were called giants.

Sigismund. What then do you think about Merlin of Britain, whom we mentioned above?

Ulrich. I think he was a real person.

Sigismund. Whose son?

Ulrich. Of two humans, a man and a woman.

Sigismund. But then why did his mother confess before the king of Britain that he was begotten of the seed of an incubus?

Ulrich. In my judgment the woman was in error, deceived by a demon into believing she had begotten Merlin from the seed of an incubus.

Sigismund. How then was this Merlin conceived?

98. Plautus, *Amphitryon*, act 1, lines 480–90, in *Amphitryon: Three Plays in New Verse Translations*, trans. Charles E. Passage and James H. Mantinband (Chapel Hill: University of North Carolina Press, 1973), 61.

Ulrich. Perhaps it happened because Merlin's mother had unfortunately given herself to the Devil, and so the Devil abused her imagination, as we have discussed already, and enchanted her senses, making as though he had sex with her, and he then perhaps made her body swell by means of an illusion, as if she were heavy with child, and when the time came for her false childbearing, with divine permission on account of the woman's unfaithfulness, he brought about a wind in her body, making her think she had been pregnant and was giving birth. Then the Devil, with divine permission on account of the woman's unfaithfulness, brought about a pain in her womb and expelled the wind, and took a child stolen from some other person and by his mysterious illusion made it appear that this child had been born from this woman. Then the mother took him, thinking he had come from her body, and brought him up, although this child had been born from other people and snatched away by the Devil.

Sigismund. Yes, I hear that the Devil is able to snatch a child away from one person and carry it to another place, giving it to another person.

Ulrich. He can do that, with God's permission, and he is especially able to snatch away unbaptized children.

Sigismund. Can you provide an example or authority to support that?

Ulrich. That the Devil has power over an unbaptized child is shown by the authority of the *Decretum*, in the chapter *Postea* and in the chapter *Sacerdotes*: "When priests place their hands on believers for the purpose of exorcism and forbid the malign spirit from dwelling within their minds, what are they doing but casting out the demons?" Likewise the text in the chapter *De hinc* in the same distinction says, "Again the Devil is exorcised, so that, acknowledging his iniquity, and fearing the just judgment of God against him, he may withdraw from the person, and from then on he may not strive to harm him with his art."[99] Notice that the Devil by his art is able to cause harm to unbaptized children. This is how I would explain the offspring and children

99. *Decretum*, pt. 3, dist. 4, chaps. 66–67, in *CIC*, vol. 1, col. 1384.

popularly thought begotten of a woman by the knight at Cologne, as we have recounted more fully in the story given above.

Sigismund. But tell me, please, who you think that unknown knight was.

Ulrich. I take him for an incubus and a devil.

Sigismund. Who do you think the sons were?

Ulrich. Saving the judgment of wiser minds, I think they were true humans snatched away from someone and brought there, as we have discussed.

Sigismund. Who then do you think the woman was, who, as we have discussed, was caught in the sea by a citizen of Sicily and taken as his wife?

Ulrich. A succubus, which is to say a devil.

Sigismund. Who do you think the son was, to whom she is supposed to have given birth, and whom she later took in the sea?

Ulrich. A devil appearing in the form of a child. For as Helinand says in the same story, "If this boy had been a true human, there is no doubt that after the mother snatched him in the sea and he drowned the sea would have cast his cadaver back onto shore, but that did not happen, since the boy disappeared and was seen no more, although it is the nature of the sea to cast all cadavers back onto the shore."

Sigismund. But many believe, don't they, that the Devil in the form of a succubus can have sex with a man and take his seed, then in the form of an incubus transmit it to a woman, generating offspring that way?

Ulrich. It does not seem to me possible, even though sperm could be collected and transmitted this way, because this does not suffice for generation. As Conciliator [i.e., Pietro da Abano] says, "You should know that that member, namely, the testicles, is not the governing factor in generative power, although such power is in it, as Galen believes, because it cannot work by itself, unless it is tempered in quantity and quality by the spirit emitted by the heart, so it is the power of the heart, which measures out this heat so that it can achieve its functions, which is the main generative power, and the power in this member [the testicles] is subservient to it, and if it has any governing function it is of this subservient kind."[100] Thus it seems to me on the basis of that theory that since the Devil cannot take from the heart that controlling spirit and that power of generation, it is clear that even if he perhaps takes the sperm from an ejaculation nothing can be generated without the other factors concomitant with that sperm.

Sigismund. From what has been said above and what has been concluded, I see it is established that such children either are fantasms or have been stolen from elsewhere and exchanged.

Ulrich. You have it just right, and Vincent seems to incline in that direction, in his *Natural History.*[101]

EPILOGUE

Sigismund. So now we have had enough discussion about this matter among ourselves. To ensure that our conclusions are firmly planted in the memory, it would be good now if you could endeavor to restate them concisely in an epilogue.

Ulrich. Let me then say as much as I can, saving the judgment of teachers with wiser insight, to whose decisions I willingly submit myself.

The first conclusion I draw is that the Devil cannot harm the elements, humans, or animals, either by himself or with the aid of humans, or make humans impotent for procreation, except when the judgment of God, which is mysterious but never unjust, allows him, whether for the punishment of our sins, or for the increase of merit through our temptation, or to bring us to fear and worship all the

---

100. Petrus de Abano, *Conciliator differentiarum philosophorum et medicorum*, differentia 35 (Venice: Luceantonius de Giunta, 1520), fol. 51ʳ, col. b.

101. *SN*, bk. 2, chap. 128, cols. 157–58.

more the glory of God's majesty, or for some other cause, as God's most gracious kindness moves him.

The second conclusion is that when God's providence, in the mysterious judgment of his goodness, allows the Devil power to harm, the Devil cannot extend this power further than has been granted him by almighty God.

The third conclusion is that, although with the permission of divine graciousness, on account of human disbelief or for some other reason discussed above, the Devil can enchant the eyes and interfere in the other human senses, so that people believe they are somewhere other than where they are, or see things not as they really are, or cause something to appear other than it is, he cannot truly change a human or animal into another species.

The fourth conclusion is that these evil women do not travel over the space of many miles in the dead of night, or gather together when they have thus traveled. Rather, while they are sleeping, or laboring under a vigorous imagination, as discussed above, the Devil impresses on them the illusory likeness of such things.[102] These and other things thus appear to them, which later when they are awake they believe in their delusion actually happened to them.

The fifth conclusion is that the Devil is by no means able to beget children, whether as an incubus or as a succubus. If such children are found, they are either exchanged or fantasms.

The sixth conclusion is that God alone has sure knowledge of future things, and he alone knows the thoughts of humans, and the Devil is not able to predict true and future things by himself or through magicians or sorcerers, except those things which by the subtlety of his nature he knows are to happen judging from his consideration of the stars and the disposition of the elements, or which by God's permission he intends to carry out,[103] or which is has incited humans to do, persuading them by putting suggestions in their minds, or which he is able to anticipate by conjecture from people's behavior and gestures, and even so he often deceives and is deceived.

---

102. Latin: *representrationem specierum similitudinarium.*

103. Reading *intendit* for *incendit.*

The seventh conclusion is that, although these accursed women can bring nothing to achievement, still at the Devil's instigation such women—whether from desperation or poverty, or from hatred of their neighbors, or on account of temptations set to them by the Devil which they do not resist—depart from the true and most gracious Lord, dedicating themselves to the Devil, worshiping him, making sacrifices and offerings to the Devil, thus apostatizing and falling into heretical depravity.

And thus follows the final conclusion, that, on account of this apostasy and corrupt will, by civil law these wicked women, who have apostatized from the most generous God and dedicated themselves to the Devil, deserve to be punished by death, as is stated in the law about sorcerers and astrologers.[104]

Therefore, O women, be mindful of your profession made in baptism, and when the Devil tempts you be strong and resist his suggestions. And in resisting arm yourselves with the sign of the cross, knowing that he has no power against you, for against this sign no peril can stand. Take as an example Saint Justina, whose legend runs as follows:[105] "There was a virgin in the city of Antioch named Justina, whom a student named Agladius often saw going to church, and he fell in love with her. Sending many envoys to her he sought her for his wife, but she said to all that she had betrothed herself to Christ, her heavenly bridegroom. Gathering a multitude of men, he sought to abduct her by force, but he was unable. Enraged, he went to Cyprian the magician, promising him two talents of gold if he could ensnare Justina with his bewitchments. By magical arts he summoned a demon, saying, 'I am in love with a young woman from among the Galileans [i.e., the Christians]. Can you win her over and bring her to me?' He promised, saying, 'Take this magic powder and sprinkle it around her house, then I will come and she will submit to me as if with filial devotion.' When Cyprian had done that, the holy virgin rose up at the third hour of the night to pray, but sensed the demon's

---

104. *Codex Iustinianus*, bk. 9, tit. 18, *De maleficis et mathemativis et ceteris similibus*, in *Corpus iuris civilis*, vol. 2, ed. Paul Krueger (Berlin: Weidmann, 1915), 379–80.

105. *SH*, bk. 12, chaps. 119–20, pp. 492–93.

assault, so she made the sign of the cross on herself and her house, and blew away the demon with the sign of the cross. He came to Cyprian, confounded. Cyprian asked why he had not brought the virgin, and he said, 'I saw some kind of sign, and I lost my strength.' Again Cyprian summoned another and stronger demon with his magic art, and he did the same thing, and the same thing happened to him. Finally he summoned the very father of the demons, and he said to him, 'How do you account for this weakness of yours? All your strength is overcome by a virgin.' The Devil replied, 'This time I will bring her to you to fulfill your lustful desire—just you be ready.' Then the Devil went in to Justina in the form of a virgin, and sitting on her bed tempted her, saying, 'I have been sent to you today by Christ to live with you in chastity, but I see that you are much tormented by your abstinence.' The holy virgin said, 'The reward is great, the effort little.' The Devil said to her, 'God in Paradise blessed Adam and Eve, saying: Increase and multiply. I fear that if we remain in virginity we will incur judgment, because we despise the word of God.' Disturbed, the virgin rose up and sensed in her spirit who it was who was speaking to her. By signing herself with the sign of the cross, she blew away the Devil, and he vanished. Then the Devil appeared to Cyprian, confounded. He said to him, 'So you, too, have been conquered, like the others who are subject to you. How have you been overcome by a Christian virgin? Tell me, what is the strength by which she has gained this victory?' He replied, 'I cannot tell you. I saw some terrible sign, and I lost all my power. But if you wish to learn the powers of this sign, swear to me that you will never leave me.' He swore, and the Devil said to him, 'I saw the sign of the Crucified, and I lost my power and melted away like wax before the fire.' Cyprian said to him, 'And so the Crucified is greater than you.' He replied, 'Indeed, he is greater than all, because those who turn away from God receive from him the sentence of [eternal] fire.' Cyprian said, 'I shall make haste, then, to became a friend of the Crucified, lest I incur such a punishment!' The Devil replied, 'But you have sworn yourself to me.' Cyprian said, 'I despise you and all your vaporous powers, and I withdraw myself from you, and crossing myself, I say: 'Glory to you, O Christ!' and 'You, O demon, depart from me!' Confounded, the Devil went away." And so Cyprian became a Christian. Take note, therefore, how much power the sign of the cross had then and has also today, the sign by which Christ deigned to mark us—Christ, who deigned to offer himself for us on the wood of the cross for our salvation, and who lives and reigns, blessed unto ages of ages. Amen.

O most glorious prince, accept then the disputation contained in this treatise, which I have worked out for the honor of Your Excellency and for the enlightenment of good minds, subject to the correction of your highness. And if you find anything inadequately worked out, or anything deviating from the path of truth, ascribe it to my ignorance rather than to presumption, and graciously receive me as your humble and faithful servant. Farewell, then, O blessed everlasting splendor of the fatherland, most venerable prince, beloved by God and by all the people. From Constance, on the tenth day of January, in the year of our Lord 1489.

The humble counselor and servant of your highness
Ulrich Molitoris of Constance, doctor of canon law, et cetera.

SELECTED BIBLIOGRAPHY

The following works will provide broader context for the study of Hartlieb and Molitoris. More specialized literature is given in the notes.

Bailey, Michael D. "The Disenchantment of Magic: Spells, Charms, and Superstition in Early European Witchcraft Literature." *American Historical Review* 111, no. 2 (2006): 383–404.

———. *Fearful Spirits, Reasoned Follies: The Boundaries of Superstition in Late Medieval Europe.* Ithaca, N.Y.: Cornell University Press, 2013.

———. "From Sorcery to Witchcraft: Clerical Conceptions of Magic in the Late Middle Ages." *Speculum* 76, no. 4 (2001): 960–90.

———. "A Late-Medieval Crisis of Superstition?" *Speculum* 84, no. 3 (2009): 633–61.

———. "Witchcraft, Superstition, and Astrology in the Late Middle Ages." In *Chasses aux sorcières et démonologie: Entre discours et pratiques (XIVe–XVIIe siècles)*, edited by Martine Ostorero, Georg Modestin, and Kathrin Utz Tremp, 349–66. Florence: SISMEL, 2010.

Cameron, Euan. *Enchanted Europe: Superstition, Reason, and Religion, 1250–1750.* New York: Oxford University Press, 2010.

———. "For Reasoned Faith or Embattled Creed? Religion for the People in Early Modern Europe." *Transactions of the Royal Historical Society*, 6th ser., 8 (1998): 165–87.

Cohn, Norman. *Europe's Inner Demons: An Enquiry Inspired by the Great Witch-Hunt.* Rev. ed. London: Chatto, 1993.

———. *Europe's Inner Demons: The Demonization of Christians in Medieval Christendom.* London: Pimlico, 1975.

Kieckhefer, Richard. "The First Wave of Trials for Diabolical Witchcraft." In *The Oxford Handbook of Witchcraft in Early Modern Europe and Colonial America*, ed. Brian P. Levack, 159–79. Oxford, UK: Oxford University Press, 2013.

―――. "Magic and Its Hazards in the Late Medieval West." In *The Oxford Handbook of Witchcraft in Early Modern Europe and Colonial America*, edited by Brian P. Levack, 13–31. Oxford, UK: Oxford University Press, 2013.

―――. *Magic in the Middle Ages.* Cambridge, UK: Cambridge University Press, 1989.

Rapisarda, Stefano, and Erik Niblaeus, eds. *Dialogues Among Books in Medieval Western Magic and Divination.* Florence: SISMEL, 2014.

Stephens, Walter. *Demon Lovers: Witchcraft, Sex, and the Crisis of Belief.* Chicago: University of Chicago Press, 2001.

Stokes, Laura Patricia. *Demons of Urban Reform: Early European Witch Trials and Criminal Justice, 1430–1530.* New York: Palgrave Macmillan, 2011.

Veenstra, J. R. *Magic and Divination at the Courts of Burgundy and France: Text and Context of Laurens Pignon's "Contre les devineurs" (1411).* Leiden: Brill, 1998.

INDEX